Conversations
with Bella

Conversations
with Bella

A LOVE STORY,
a SPIRITUAL ODYSSEY,
and the GIFT
of a BROKEN HEART

By Merv Dickinson

With a Foreword by Kenneth Ring

Inner Connexions
Christchurch, New Zealand

Published by Inner Connexions Publishing Limited, Christchurch, New Zealand 8053

For more information or permission requests, contact
Inner Connexions Publishing Limited at innerconnexionsnz@yahoo.com

Published 2018.
ISBN-13: 978-0-473-43742-8 (paperback)
ISBN-13: 978-0-473-43743-5 (e-book)

A catalogue record for this book is available from the National Library of New Zealand.
National Library of New Zealand Cataloguing-in-Publications Data
Dickinson, John Mervyn, 1934 –
Conversations with Bella: a love story, a spiritual odyssey, and the gift of a broken heart/Merv Dickinson
Includes bibliographical references.
ISBN 978-0-473-43742-8 (paperback) | ISBN 978-0-473-43743-5 (e-book)
Subjects: 1. Biography/autobiography
National Library of New Zealand record available at https://natlib.govt.nz/

THEY CAN'T TAKE THAT AWAY FROM ME
(from "Shall We Dance")

Cover and interior design by Angie Dickinson Design. Contact angiedesign@me.com.
Editing by Riça Night. Contact msgodedit@gmail.com.

To Bella, my sweet darling,
with undying love and gratitude
for sharing this life with me.

~ CONTENTS ~

$\sim$ ACKNOWLEDGEMENTS $\sim$

W riting this book has been so much a part of my grief process over these two-plus years since Bella died that it is scarcely possible to distinguish one from the other. Friends who supported me in my grief supported and encouraged me in my writing as well. And those who assisted me in bringing this book to publication did so with gentleness and sensitivity to my grief. I am immensely grateful to them all.

Living on my own in New Zealand now, with all remaining family scattered across the world, my personal support while writing this book came chiefly from a small Men's Group that met every second Sunday evening. Just five of us—David Goldsmith, Martin Lewis, Bill Packard, Nick Williamson, and me—shared with each other the deepest and most intimate aspects of our lives. And not only on Sunday evenings, but on scheduled mornings each week when two or three of us got together over coffee for stimulating conversation as we set about solving the problems of the world. Each of these friends is hugely intelligent, deeply respectful, and wise enough to know that none of us has "the truth," as together we explore wherever our personal experience and insatiable curiosity takes us.

On countless occasions, at the risk of seeming crazy, I shared with these friends the astonishing inner experiences I was having in the wake of Bella's death. And I was invariably met, not with kindly condescension, but with a genuine desire to hear and understand what was happening to me. Despite declaring themselves to be either atheists or agnostics, each of these friends has a distinctly spiritual interest. David and Nick each have a history of Zen practice. Martin has been steeped in personal growth work. And Bill was blown away, many years ago, when for ten full days he unexpectedly found himself in an altered state of consciousness that had all the characteristics of enlightenment.

At one of our Men's Group meetings, several weeks after Bella died, I hesitantly shared with these friends some of my journal notes in which I had recorded my experiences of Bella's continuing presence and some of the "messages" I had received, as if from her, in a practice that I call "deep listening." Far from dismissing my experience as absurd, they suggested that I consider sharing it in writing—in a book that David thought could be titled *Conversations with Bella*.

So thanks, guys, for your friendship, support, and encouragement, without which I would never have embarked on this writing project.

Thanks, too, to Jenny Wade and Kenneth Ring—friends and colleagues in the San Francisco Bay area. Jenny is an internationally known researcher in consciousness studies and developmental psychology, currently Professor of Integral and Transpersonal Psychology at the California Institute of Integral Studies in San Francisco. Her 1996 book *Changes of Mind: A Holonomic Theory of the Evolution of Consciousness* (Albany, NY: SUNY Press) was seminal in shaping my thinking several years ago. Ken is also internationally recognized for his study of near-death experiences, for his several books on the subject, and for his co-founding of the International Association for Near-Death Studies. He is Professor Emeritus of Psychology at the University of Connecticut.

In late 2016, in an e-mail exchange with Jenny regarding one of her papers that had been uploaded to an academic website—www.academia.edu —of which I am a member, I shared with her some of my own grief experiences that seemed relevant to our discussion. She immediately responded, saying she was "ravished" by the way I wrote about the gift of a broken heart, and asked if she might forward my e-mails to her friend Kenneth Ring. She thought he might be interested in how grief can open the door to quasi-mystical experiences. He in turn quickly responded with his own encouragement. "I am delighted," he wrote, "to know you are thinking of publishing your experiences, and indeed think your book will be a solace and inspiration to many. I think you're onto something, another of those under-the-radar experiences nobody has talked about but that may be more common than we imagine."

I have since enjoyed an ongoing friendship with Ken, who, in addition to his personal support and encouragement, agreed to contribute a foreword to this book.

So to you, Jenny and Ken, my heartfelt thanks. You have each been a gift to me and have influenced my life more than I expect you know.

And then there is my editor, Riça Night. I first met Riça forty years ago, but we had lost track of each other at some point in the intervening years. A few months ago, she noticed my name on LinkedIn and sent me a "Hi, how are you" message. In the exchange that followed, she learned that I had all but completed the manuscript for this book, and I learned that she had spent the past few decades of her life as a professional editor. What ensued was a working relationship without which this book would not have seen the light of day. I had previously written only academic papers, and it was a challenge to maintain the intensely personal style of a memoir. So I am hugely appreciative of Riça's skilled editorial eye, astonishing thoroughness, and steady commitment to helping bring this book to birth. Whether she was sent to me by heaven or whether her reappearance in my life was entirely serendipitous may never be known.

Finally, my thanks to my daughter-in-law, Angie Dickinson. She and my son Bruce live in Atlanta, Georgia, where she works as a graphic designer with all the artistic and technical skills required to design this book's cover and interior. But what most of all she brought to the task was her love of Bella. Whenever they had occasion to be together, they played outrageously. So thank you, Angie. I know that your contribution to this book has been, for you, as it has for me, a labour of love.

JUNE 2018   MERV DICKINSON, PH.D.

∾ FOREWORD ∾

Kenneth Ring, Ph.D., is Professor Emeritus of Psychology at the University of Connecticut and an internationally recognized authority on near-death experiences (NDEs). Regarded as the "Dean of NDE Researchers," he is cofounder and past president of the International Association for Near-Death Studies and the founding editor of its quarterly publication, Journal of Near-Death Studies. *He is the author of several books on NDEs, including* Life at Death: A Scientific Investigation of the Near-Death Experience *(1980),* Heading Toward Omega: In Search of the Meaning of the Near-Death Experience *(1984),* The Omega Project: Near-Death Experiences, UFO Encounters, and Mind at Large *(1992),* Lessons from the Light: What We Can Learn from the Near-Death Experience *(1998), and* Mindsight: Near-Death and Out-of-Body Experiences in the Blind *(1999).*

An ordinary spring day. Merv Dickinson and Bella, his wife of fifty years, have just finished breakfast. He starts checking e-mail; she goes into their bedroom to get dressed. As she passes him, he asks reflexively how she is. She replies, "Fine." He returns to his e-mail. She does not return.

"Fine." That will be the last word Merv hears spoken by his beloved Bella. It has one meaning in English, but another in music, where it means "the end." How could he know—how could she have known—which of these meanings that word portended?

He never hears her fall. But he finds her on the bedroom floor, unconscious. Just like that, with no warning. One moment she is "fine"; the next, she is dying. Then dead.

Merv is shocked, stunned, shattered—completely devastated. No chance to say goodbye. Too late now for everything but tears.

But then comes something that is even more of a surprise. An unexpected blessing that, like Bella's death, will completely change his life: the gift of a broken heart.

Let me quote Merv's words, for they will tell you directly what he felt in the moments immediately after Bella's death:

> [A]s I knelt beside the bed, my dismay was swallowed up in a tidal wave of love. Nothing less than a tsunami of love poured through my broken heart. It was a love beyond anything I had ever known. A love so immense that I knew it wasn't my love but a love that fills the universe. A love at the heart of the universe. Of which my own expressions of love are a meagre trickle. But now, somehow, this breaking of my heart had opened the floodgates and allowed a previously dammed-up ocean of love to engulf me. Together, Bella and I were drowning in an ocean of love. In fact, *that's what we are. That's what we* all *are*. We are individual expressions of that love. We are waves on an ocean of love.

Most of my own professional work has dealt with the study of near-death experiences (NDEs). In the course of this work, which spanned over thirty years, I have heard words like these many times from those who have temporarily crossed over the barrier that separates life from death. Here's just one example, from a woman named Peggy who is describing what she experienced after she encountered an all-loving light:

> *I vividly recall the part where the light did what felt like switch on a current of pure, undiluted, concentrated unconditional LOVE. This love I experienced in the light was so powerful it can't be compared to earthly love, even though earthly love is a much milder version. It's like knowing that the very best love you feel on earth is diluted to about one part per million of the real thing. … I remember being loved by the light. It never once stopped loving me and I'll never forget the impression this made on me. I thought, "There is more love here than anything else … ." It was like being bathed in energy particles of pure love. … The light told me everything was Love, and I mean everything!*

This is what the encounter with death—whether one's own or that of a loved one—can reveal, and it is indeed a soul-shattering revelation. What the individual who is granted this experience comes to realize is that the universe itself seems to be pulsating with an unimaginably powerful current of pure love and that this current can sometimes be directly transmitted to that individual.

This was Bella's gift to Merv. She was Jewish, so one might say this was her supreme *mitzvah* to him, her parting gift, the gift that came from her parting because by doing so, she broke her husband's heart, and only when it was broken could the Love come bursting through.

Still, Merv is initially sunk in his grief. His life with his beloved Bella meant everything to him. Without her physical presence, he is bereft. But as he had long ago formed the habit of daily meditation, he initiates a process that he calls "deep listening," in which he tries to enter into the silence of his mind, ignoring or stilling the everyday chatter, and simply trying to be open to whatever emerges.

And one day, he hears the voice of Bella in his mind. This is the first part of the message he receives:

Hello, you.

All is very well.
My transition was beautiful—very "Bella."
You need have nothing to fear.
I will not leave you—ever.
That is impossible. We are one.

Love is different here.
It doesn't ebb and flow; it's not a feeling; it just is.
I love you now with complete steadiness,
and will be with you always.
You need only "look up" and you will know that I am here.

After suffering the death of a loved one, many people have some kind of presentiment of them, some unmistakable sign that they still exist. In almost all cases of this sort—they are called after-death communications (ADCs)—what is communicated is very similar to the message that Merv received. The surviving person is given to understand that the deceased person is well and continues to love and care for the one who has been left behind. These messages are usually very convincing to those who receive them, especially when the deceased person is actually seen (sometimes by other witnesses as well).

Nevertheless, it is rare that the person who has died appears to communicate telepathically to the survivor a *series* of such messages over a considerable period of time. But that is indeed the case with Merv, which is why he titled this memoir *Conversations with Bella* (even if the conversations were largely one-sided). And most of these messages take a similar form—conveying reassurance, love, and the promise of a continuing connection that will never be broken.

Merv comes to feel that his continuing grief is his love line to Bella; he doesn't ever want to cut the connection lest he lose contact with her. Besides, he understands that grief and love are inextricably conjoined. Grief, he writes, is "just another word for love. And I don't want either to end." And, again, "I don't *want* my broken heart to heal."

But what are we to make of these messages? Are they *really* from Bella, or are they simply grief-generated consolations that Merv has somehow allowed to well up from his unconscious during his meditations?

Throughout much of the memoir, Merv himself struggles with this conundrum. The rational, skeptical part of him is inclined not to take them as literal evidence of Bella's continued existence, and yet his heart yearns to believe they are authentic and not just self-created. How can one know with certainty how they should be regarded? It seems impossible to say.

Yet here we may recall Pascal's famous dictum: "The heart has its reasons which reason knows nothing of. ...We know the truth not only by the reason but also by the heart."°*

This at least offers us a way to resolve the dilemma. The head gives

---

* The degree symbol shown here is used throughout this book to signal that you can find further information, such as citations for quotes and paraphrases, in the Notes section that starts on page 163.

us knowledge; the heart affords us *gnosis*—access to the realm of the transcendent to which reason alone is barred.

But if the heart can become the gateway to the transcendent realm in which the spirits of our loved ones may reside, by what means can we establish contact with this invisible world? One answer to this question, which Merv himself hits upon, at least as a hypothesis, lies in a proper understanding of the imagination.

Here, the term is not meant in the ordinary sense of something we dream up in a reverie or while writing a novel when we invent fictional characters to further the plot. No, it is more akin to the way the apostles of the imagination, such as Blake and Coleridge, used it, as a creative power in its own right that can be used to penetrate into the invisible world that lies beyond that of our sense-based reality.

Merv has had the same insight and puts it very eloquently: "Imagination may not simply be a fanciful view of things, adopted in this case for my comfort in the absence of hard evidence, but a means of reaching out to a transcendent Mystery that, by its very nature, is inaccessible to our ordinary mode of rational or sensible knowing."

Exactly.

In the same way that Freud argued that dreams are the royal road to the unconscious, so we might say that imagination, in the sense that both Merv and I are using it here, is the golden bridge to the transcendent.

Heart or head? Messages from Bella's spirit or from Merv's mind? Which do you choose? My suggestion: Stop reading this foreword—at least in a few minutes—and read the memoir instead. Then decide.

It's neither my intention nor my charge to do more than provide a kind of introduction to the memoir you're about to read, and in a few moments I will be inviting you to do just that. But I would be remiss if I didn't tell you just a bit more about the author and what you will find in his beautifully crafted memoir.

Merv Dickinson, now in his early eighties, was during his working life a man who wore many hats. After obtaining his Ph.D. in psychology, he worked at various times as a therapist, an organizational consultant, a restaurateur, a university lecturer, and a minister—but throughout his life he has been drawn to pursue a deep spiritual interest. He is a lover of poetry and of trees, and you will find his book strewn with wonderful poems and abundant evidence of his spiritual discernment.

As his subtitle implies, this memoir brings together three intertwining themes—his and Bella's love story, his spiritual journey, and, most important, how these culminated in the gift of a broken heart.

In weaving together these threads, Merv takes you into the past when Bella was alive as well as into his experience of the two years immediately after her death—the story of his grief and what it led to, about which I will say nothing more apart from this: you will not be disappointed. You will learn about his quotidian life—and a good deal about his innermost life. By the end of the book, you will know him—and Bella—very well.

Just a word of advice and a personal comment. Like many people, I have read any number of books describing how it feels to lose a beloved spouse, and have always found them moving. But Merv writes such luminous prose and with such profound spiritual wisdom that, even though this is a short book, I suggest you read it slowly and with care. It is worth savoring; it merits and rewards a thoughtful reading.

In thinking about Merv's story, I found myself remembering some of the words of France's second-most-famous woman saint and religious visionary, Simone Weil. In speaking of the crushing blows that can leave a man utterly forlorn and in the depths of a seemingly irremediable despair, she nevertheless sees something very much like what Merv has discovered for himself. Weil uses religious language that Merv himself avoids (despite his work as a minister), but she points to what Merv found at the end of his own journey:

> The man who has known pure joy, if only for a moment ... is the only man for whom affliction is something devastating. ... But, after all, for him it is no punishment; it is God holding his hand and pressing rather hard. For, if he remains constant, what he will discover buried deep under the sound of his own lamentations is the pearl of the silence of God.

NOVEMBER 2017   KENNETH RING, PH.D.

～ INTRODUCTION ～
THEMES THAT SHAPE OUR STORY

There's nothing quite like facing death to lift the lid from a Pandora's box of unanswerable questions. Or open the door to experiences I would never have thought possible. Except perhaps being in the presence of a newborn child. Hugely different occasions! One, an anguished breaking open of my heart. The other, an up-close encounter with an innocence I have lost. Each delivering a sense of wonder at the miracle and mystery of it all.

Both experiences were given to me recently. And changed my life.

I first met Kai, my youngest grandson, when he was ten weeks old. He lives in Sydney, a three-hour flight from my New Zealand home. His name means *sea* in Japanese. He was born on October 16, 2016, exactly one year to the day after Bella—my lover, partner, wife, and best friend of almost fifty years—died suddenly and unexpectedly.

> One generation passes away, and another generation comes; ... All the rivers run into the sea; ... To the place from which the rivers come, there they return again.°*

For me, and certainly for Kai, our meeting was a novel experience. I have three other grandchildren—Mitch, Kayla, and Christopher—but they are thirty-something now, and I never knew them as children. I was always somewhere else, pursuing whatever adventure was current. Too far away to have contact with them—and, without that contact, to feel anything remotely

---

* The degree symbol shown here is used throughout this book to signal that you can find further information, such as citations for quotes and paraphrases, in the Notes section that starts on page 163.

grandfatherly. Indeed, whenever I had seen others of my vintage exclaiming over their grandchildren, I had wondered if perhaps I lacked the grandfather gene. So I was eager, and a little anxious lest I fail the test, to find out what my meeting with Kai would be like.

What I, and perhaps we, discovered was a delightfully surprising and surprisingly delightful connection. To soothe him during what seemed his regularly scheduled early evening crying time, I did what fifty-plus years ago I had done with each of my own three sons. I sang to him. Silly, playful, light-hearted songs from another era, like Nat King Cole's "Orange Colored Sky"° and Perry Como's "Hot Diggity (Dog Ziggity Boom)."° He liked that. He would smile, make a kind of cooing sound—which I understood to mean "Isn't this fun?"—and sometimes laugh. Actual laughter from this ten-week-old being! And I would laugh too. I took this to be what is meant by *bonding*.

What should not have been surprising was my sense of wonder at the miracle of life. How can any thoughtful person *not* feel wonder in the presence of a newborn? But it was new for me. Or at least so long ago in my experience that I had forgotten. I mean, here is this tiny being, perfectly formed, with ten fingers and ten toes and more than eighty-five billion neurons already learning Japanese when his mother speaks to him and English when he hears his father's voice. It's the product, I am told, of instructions encoded in DNA molecules for how to turn amino acids into proteins and bring them all together over nine months into the astonishing architecture of the human body.

But beyond the miracle of pregnancy and birth, I find myself marvelling at the wonder of a life yet to unfold. In my interactions with Kai, it seemed obvious that someone was at home. I know it's no longer fashionable to think that we possess a soul. "There is no soul," declared Francis Crick, who codiscovered the structure of the DNA molecule. "You, your joys and your sorrows, your memories and your ambitions, your sense of personal identity and free will, are in fact no more than the behaviour of a vast assembly of nerve cells and their associated molecules."° Well, maybe. And then again, maybe not. At least I have yet to meet anyone who does not act *as if* someone is at home. Certainly, I had no doubt that packaged in Kai's little body is *a point of consciousness* that one day will call itself "I."

As together we smiled and laughed and made "goo-goo" noises, I couldn't help wondering who this tiny being really is. A point of consciousness, a locus of awareness, yes! But still with no *world*. Just a booming, buzzing cacophony of sensory impressions, out of which will gradually emerge *Kai's world*. Mommy, Daddy, and Grandpa Merv. Kangaroos, kookaburras, and koalas. "The whole *megillah*," as Bella would have said. And with that a *self*. No longer immersed in the oneness of it all, but standing forth as a separate being named Kai. "I" will become clothed in "me." Self-awareness time! Separation time! He will emerge out of oneness into what the Taoist sage Lao Tzu called the world of "ten thousand things"°—and with it, he will inherit all the wonder and joy and sorrow and suffering that is our human birthright.

As I looked at Kai, and sang to and laughed with him, he seemed to be a bundle of potential waiting to unfold. Or perhaps a yet-unpublished story waiting to be lived. The broad outline has already been written simply because he is human. He will become Kai. He will develop a personality, a self-image, an ego. Hopefully he will learn to think well of himself. When he is flying high, he may, as I did, think he is the cat's pyjamas. And later he may come to see the absurdity of these ego-pretensions and begin to wonder who he *really* is. Soon enough, he will face his mortality and know that he will die. One day, almost certainly, he will fall in love. And at some point, however fleetingly, he may ask the Big Questions, the unanswerable questions that human beings have pondered for millennia. *What am I doing here? Is there any purpose to it all? Is there something I am meant to be doing with my life?* Or is it, as Macbeth lamented, "a tale told by an idiot, full of sound and fury/ Signifying nothing"?°

Could it be that, beyond this broad outline, more specific themes may yet be waiting to unfold? They may simply evolve, shaped by events that befall him and his responses to those events. Or perhaps they are already written. Are we the author of our life's story? Or is it shaped, as many have believed, by what preceded it in former lifetimes? Perhaps this lifetime is just a one-semester course, with its own curriculum, in which we learn what we need to learn en route to our eventual graduation.

I can't help wondering about such things. How is it possible *not* to wonder? It seems I've been wondering all my life. My wonder is usually eclipsed by all the everyday concerns I take so seriously. It's easy to lose perspective. But then along come days like these when I find myself in the presence of a newborn child. Awakening me once more to wonder, and to ask the questions I can neither answer nor avoid.

∾

Those days with Kai also prompted me to reflect on my own life story. Which after more than eighty years is easier than when I was immersed in its earlier chapters. And as I did, two themes came into focus.

One is a lifelong and still-ongoing *opening more and more to love.* Following the metaphor of life as a required one-semester course, "Learning to Love" has been a core subject in my curriculum. God knows, it has not been easy. I've made huge mistakes. But then, that's how we learn. And given to me as a mentor, to suffer with me through it all, was Bella. The course has played out as a very human *love story* that runs throughout this memoir. An adventurous, tumultuous, often-painful story of finding our way through betrayal and forgiveness—opening, resisting, and opening again to an ever-deepening love.

The second theme is another still-ongoing process. One of *self-discovery.* Or more accurately, of "*Self-remembering,*" to use the term coined by the Armenian mystic G.I. Gurdjieff.° I can't say when this quest began. But by my late teens, it was a recognizable theme. I was never driven by any desire to be rich or famous. Only to understand the mystery of what it means to be fully human. So I studied philosophy and theology and finally psychology before realizing that the answers I am looking for will not be found in books or classrooms, but in my own inner experience—in what is still playing out as *a spiritual odyssey.*

I have no sense of having chosen either theme. *Learning to love* and *Self-remembering* are not electives in my life's curriculum. They are core requirements. I may have said yes to them at some level, but I didn't consciously *choose* them. Childhood influences no doubt shaped the curriculum. Mutations of themes already playing out in the lives of my parents. But what I find intriguing is how these themes intertwine. Like baroque fugues, each builds on and reinforces the other. The love story and the spiritual odyssey are inseparable. One cannot be told without the other.

And at the heart of each has been, and still is, my beloved Bella.

But most astonishing, and why I've written this memoir, is that these themes together culminate in *the gift of a broken heart*. Delivered on that October morning, the year before Kai was born, when Bella died. A gift that continues to disclose ever-deeper levels of who I am and what it means to love, and so dramatically completes both the love story and the spiritual odyssey that I wonder if perhaps it is a God-sent or Bella-sent preparation for sitting my final exams.

Writing this memoir may well be an attempt to complete what those who know about such things would call my *grief work*. An attempt to digest all that has happened, integrate it into my life, and "move on," as people like to say. But whatever the motive, it's something I must do. *Not* to write this account is quite impossible. I need to acknowledge and say "thank you" to whatever gods may be for the gift of Bella in my life—for the love story and the spiritual odyssey that we have shared, and for this astonishing gift of a broken heart.

I don't for a moment intend to suggest that your experience of grief, dear reader, should be like mine. All the tips-on-grieving handbooks make clear that there is no right way to grieve. But if anything in this account affirms your own experience, or proves helpful when you must say goodbye to someone you deeply love, or lets you face your own demise with greater equanimity, or opens you to gifts that may lie hidden in your grief—if it enables you to say from your own experience, now or in the future, "blessed are those who mourn"°—then my writing this memoir will have been worthwhile.

Reflecting on more than thirty years of helping people deal with grief, Stephen Levine, a gentle American teacher of Theravada Buddhism, wrote this:

> I've been with many people whose grief has been beyond bearing. And in some way it has been the best thing that ever happened to them. For they have come to plumb the depths of their being, experiencing it as an incredible opportunity to get in touch with places they would probably never have access to otherwise.°

That has been my experience precisely. Or in the exquisite words of Rashani Réa:

> There is a brokenness
> out of which comes the unbroken,
> a shatteredness
> out of which blooms the unshatterable.
>
> There is a sorrow
> beyond all grief which leads to joy
> and a fragility
> out of whose depths emerges strength.
>
> There is a hollow space
> too vast for words
> through which we pass with each loss,
> out of whose darkness
> we are sanctioned into being.
>
> There is a cry deeper than all sound
> whose serrated edges cut the heart
> as we break open to the place inside
> which is unbreakable and whole
> while learning to sing.°

That too has been my experience. And the consummate gift of a broken heart.

∾ ONE ∾
DAYS THAT CHANGE OUR LIFE

Telling stories is what we humans do. We've been doing it for millennia, since spoken language first evolved. Sitting around the campfire, or its current equivalent, sharing our experiences in the continuously updated story of our life. It's how we make sense of our life. We shape it as a story. From the myriad mostly forgotten events that befall us, we select the most memorable and weave them into themes that form the storyline that is our life. Developing along the way the character we think we are.

How or why these themes emerge and develop as they do, I don't pretend to know. Often they appear without warning. Unexpected and certainly unplanned. A day dawns that is ordinary in every respect. You shower and get dressed. You have breakfast. You start your day, embarking on whatever must be done. Usually it's quite routine and mundane. Nothing exceptional. A day like any other. And then, out of the blue, something happens that changes your life forever. Literally, changes your life forever. *Your life can never be the same again.*

This is my story. And the days that changed my life. Playful. Beatific. Devastating. Unforgettable days that launched the themes that shape the story that runs throughout my life. A love story and a spiritual odyssey playing out together and issuing most recently in the gift of a broken heart.

∾

FEBRUARY 14, 1966
It was a Monday. In Toronto. Late in the afternoon. I'd spent most of the day at the Toronto Institute of Human Relations, where I worked as Director

of Training. I was thirty-one years old. Before returning home to my wife, Carol, and our three young sons, I decided to do an hour's workout at Vic Tanny's Health Spa—the one on Eglinton Avenue just east of Yonge Street. It was not a good decision. Already it was snowing heavily. No wind. Just big fat snowflakes piling up and clogging the streets. As I was leaving, I thought, "Driving twenty miles home at rush hour in conditions like this will be a nightmare." And in that moment, a goddess appeared—a stunningly beautiful instructor and sometime receptionist at the spa who, a few months earlier, had sold me a life membership. She too was leaving. Heading home to her husband and children. Her name was Bella.

I wasn't on the make. I was going home. But I heard myself saying, as if it made perfectly good sense, "With all this snow and snarled traffic, maybe we should wait a while before heading home. Would you like to go for a drink?" She said that sounded like a good idea. So we took my 1961 Ford Falcon station wagon—a "compact" in those days—and drove a few blocks to the Ports of Call restaurant. Only recently opened, it had made a splash on the Toronto scene with its themed rooms, each representing a different and exotic "port of call." We chose the Bali Hai—a Polynesian lounge in which a tropical rainstorm occurred periodically in one corner of the room. It was a deliciously sensuous retreat from the cold and snowbound streets outside.

Of all life's myriad events, only a few are indelibly inscribed as clear and detailed memories. Are they so memorable because they launch a new chapter in our life? Or do they launch a new chapter because they are so memorable? I remember that on this occasion, because we both had yet to drive home in difficult conditions, we settled for sharing just one exotic drink. A rum-based cocktail with lime juice and Curaçao, topped with a cherry, a slice of lime, and a small bamboo parasol. It was called a Mai Tai, and it cost $1.95. We talked, we laughed, we found that we had lots in common and a few intriguing differences. And we liked each other.

I learned, for instance, that she liked Walt Whitman's poetry and had a copy of his *Leaves of Grass* in her handbag.° It became part of our library when, more than three years later, we moved in together and I discovered that, at the top of the first page, she had inscribed her own variant of a Bible verse from Song of Solomon: "My beloved has returned, and the voice of the turtle is heard once more in the land."° I like to think she was referring to me. Opposite that, on the inside front cover, are listed the ingredients for some recipe—"hard-boiled egg, parsley, spring onion, oregano, 4 drained anchovies, phyllo pastry"—and other items written so illegibly that Bella alone would know what they are.

I learned too that she had grown up in Wales, in a town called Merthyr Tydfil, named after Saint Tydfil, a daughter of King Brychan of Brycheiniog, who had been martyred (*merthyr* means "martyr" in Welsh) by marauding pagans in the 5th century. Bella had grown up there in an orthodox Jewish family that had escaped the pogroms in Russia at the end of the 19th century. I was fascinated. To my middle-class gentile ears, this was more exotic than the Mai Tai we were sipping or the tropical rainstorm in the corner of the room. In return, I tried to impress this goddess with a harrowing account of my own experiences in Alabama several months previously on the Selma-to-Montgomery civil rights march. As best I can recall, we didn't speak much of the families waiting for us in the deepening darkness of our snow-clogged city.

We both must have known that these were the first steps in a mating dance. But we didn't acknowledge it—perhaps not even to ourselves. We needed to get home to our respective families. So after about an hour in our Polynesian retreat, we drove back through the still-falling snow to where Bella's car was parked. She drove an even smaller "subcompact": a Nash Metropolitan—the same sexy two-seater model once owned by Princess Margaret and Elvis Presley. When we said goodbye, hidden behind my car's heavily snow-covered windscreen, we kissed. And then we kissed again. And from that moment, our lives would never be the same again.

Falling in love is a strange expression. But the experience *is* like that. Love is not something we choose, but something we fall into. We call it *falling* because, once started, we are powerless to stop it. We trip over something and we start to fall. We may struggle to regain our balance, but it's too late. The power of attraction, whether *gravity* or *love,* is too strong. And so it was on this snow-filled Monday afternoon in Toronto, when unexpectedly I tripped. And fell. The beginning of a new chapter. The emergence of a new theme. Was it only a coincidence that this was Valentine's Day?

~

JANUARY 1, 1980

In terms of the calendar alone, this was a noteworthy day. The first day of a new year and of a new decade. The preceding year had been less than stellar. A revolution in Iran had ousted the Shah and allowed Ayatollah Khomeini to return as supreme leader of a new Islamic Republic. A few months later, militants had seized the U.S. embassy in Tehran; they were still holding fifty-two hostages. Anthrax spores had accidentally been released from a Soviet bioweapons facility. The partial meltdown of a reactor at the Three Mile Island Nuclear Generating Station near Niagara Falls had released radioactive gases into the surrounding environment. Margaret Thatcher had become Britain's Prime Minister. And, perhaps fittingly, *Apocalypse Now* was playing at local cinemas.

Bella and I were in northern Scotland, on the coast of the Moray Firth, two months into a three-month orientation program to see if we might become members of the Findhorn Community. It was considered the flagship among the many New Age communities emerging at that time throughout Europe and America. A year earlier, Bella had accidentally come across a book titled *The Magic of Findhorn*,° which prompted us to arrange our initial visit to what then was a community of some 300 members. Now here we were on another snow-filled Monday evening, which happened to be New Year's Eve, in one of the caravans or mobile homes in which some residents lived, enjoying dinner with a group of friends.

Just before midnight, Bella and I drove into the nearby town of Forres to welcome the new year as only the Scots know how. In the town square, delighting in the fresh-falling snow, while the bagpipes swirled, we joined the gathered townsfolk in singing *Auld Lang Syne*. We didn't stay long. By 1:00 a.m. we were home—"home" being a bedroom in the sub-basement of what had once been a four-star hotel and was now one of the Community's main residences. We'd had a wonderful evening. But on this winter night, we were glad to be snug in bed.

And then it happened! In the wee hours of that New Year's morning, I was awakened by what would be one of the most profound and overwhelming spiritual experiences of my life. I'll wait until a later chapter to describe it fully. For now, suffice it to say that our bedroom was filled with a *Presence*—in light of which, with tears of gratitude streaming down my face, I *knew* beyond any doubt why we needed to be at Findhorn and what my life was to be about.

Over the ensuing weeks and months, what unfolded seemed nothing less than miraculous. A new chapter had begun. A powerful new theme had emerged that would shape my life story for the rest of my days. And my life would never be the same again. Exactly one year later, on New Year's Day 1981, Bella and I arrived in New Zealand on what felt like a tidal wave of grace.

~

OCTOBER 16, 2015

Although one can never be sure, because such events are so utterly beyond our control, I suspect that this may rightly be considered the first day of the final chapter of my life. It was a springtime morning in Christchurch—the beginning of another beautiful day in paradise. A cherry tree was in full bloom just outside the kitchen window of the two-bedroom villa into which we had moved three years earlier, in a small upmarket retirement community. We had previously lived, for many years, in the seaside suburb of Sumner. But that was thirty minutes from the nearest hospital or ambulance service. And, as the years ticked by, we thought we'd sleep more soundly knowing medical help was closer at hand. It proved to be a good decision. Our villa was spacious, sunlit, and secure. We had good friends, watchful neighbours, and three Call buttons strategically placed in different rooms to summon help if the need arose.

As it happened, the need *did* arise on this Friday morning. We had just finished breakfast. I was sitting at the dining-room table, checking my e-mail. Bella had returned her dishes to the kitchen sink and headed back to the bedroom to get dressed. Nothing was amiss. As she passed me in the dining room, I asked her how she was feeling. "Fine," she said. But two minutes later she was unconscious, slumped in the doorway between the en suite bathroom and the walk-in wardrobe. I hadn't heard her fall. Just the death rattle. I pushed a Call button. A voice from a speaker in the wall told me what to do. Within five minutes, staff from our retirement village were there. Within ten minutes, the ambulance and paramedics arrived. But it was all to no avail. Sometime within the next twenty minutes, Bella was gone. All the Call buttons in the world will not guarantee your safety.

As on each previous occasion, it had begun as just another ordinary day. And in a heartbeat—or rather, the stopping of a heartbeat—my life would never be the same again. American author Joan Didion, writing about her own grief following her husband's sudden death, described it this way: "Life changes in the instant. You sit down to dinner and life as you know it ends."° That's how it was for me. Except that it was breakfast time, not dinnertime.

Didion again: "Grief turns out to be a place none of us knows until we reach it."° Yes! What happened as I sat beside Bella's lifeless body, and what has occurred since then, took me to a place I had never been before and didn't know existed. Over the years, I have of course said goodbye to many friends and family members. If you live long enough, that goes with the territory. And each time, to varying degrees, I have felt sorrow, sometimes shock. But never anything resembling what I know now as grief. Bella and I had sometimes imagined what it would be like to say our last goodbye. The very thought would bring tears to my eyes. But nothing could have prepared me for the actual experience.

On that Friday morning, Bella's physical heart quite literally broke. In an instant, it fell apart. The coroner later said she'd suffered a cardiac rupture. And a few minutes later, my own heart broke. *My heart broke!* Another strange expression! What's the heart got to do with it? It's only a pump. Isn't it? Perhaps we say it broke because the experience *feels* so very physical. As I sat beside Bella's vacant body, holding a hand that grew colder by the minute, stroking her forehead, kissing her closed eyes, I felt as if something in the region of my heart *broke open,* releasing a tsunami of grief that was at the same time a tsunami of love.

There really are no words. What can I say? *Grief is just another word for love.* Bella was dead. I was not. And together we were *drowning in an ocean of love.*

It must sound strange to anyone who has not experienced it, but to me it was a gift. *The gift of a broken heart.* This unfathomable grief, this ultimate desolation, *opened my heart* to dimensions of love and depths of spiritual experience beyond anything I had ever known—and I suspect that I would never have known if not for this breaking of my heart. And because of it, my life can never be the same again.

Virtually every spiritual tradition speaks of the importance of an open and tender heart. Jesus repeatedly warned against the hardness of our hearts. "Be careful," said the Taoist sage Master Zhuang, "not to interfere with the natural goodness of the heart. By gentleness, the hardest heart may be softened. But try to cut and polish it, and it will freeze like ice."° "The mind creates the abyss," said the Hindu sage Nisargadatta Maharaj, "the heart crosses it."° "Their hearts were torn open,"° wrote Stephen Levine about a couple whose eleven-year-old daughter had been murdered. He went on to say:

> The tearing open of the heart leaves the heart vulnerable and exposed. ... You find yourself torn open to the truth. ...°

> It is in the tearing open of the heart that we ... see how our work is to be more loving.°

I have no idea why this should be so. I don't begin to understand the psychology, the physiology, the neurology of a broken heart. But it's absolutely true to my experience. And to me it was a gift.

~

The love story that began on a snow-filled Valentine's Day in Toronto in 1966 was the necessary prelude to the spiritual odyssey so dramatically launched on that snow-filled New Year's Eve in Scotland. And both were mystically confirmed in the breaking open of my heart on that fateful Friday morning when Bella died.

But most remarkable of all, and to me quite inexplicable, is that each of these days had one thing in common. Each was inviting me to a deeper, expanded experience of love. As if love itself was pursuing me, refusing to leave me alone, sweeping me up in wave after recurring wave until finally I might get the message: that opening to love is what, for me at least, this life is all about.

～ TWO ～
THE MORNING BELLA DIED

Bella and I were not early risers. Unlike most others in our retirement village, whose inner clocks seem set by the rhythms of Cantabrian farm life, we usually lingered in bed until the risk of being seen as sloths prompted us to at least pull back the drapes, if not to "seize the day." Bella liked the expression *Carpe diem*, and would often say it with a sleepy smile as I took my first reluctant steps out of bed. But many years had passed since either of us had to seize the day.

I was almost always the first one up, if only to open the drapes before returning to bed for what we called "a cuddle." As we'd grown older, a cuddle usually amounted to no more than that, but it was delicious nonetheless. I would ask Bella if she wanted to come into my nest, which meant snuggling into the crook of my arm, her head nestled on my chest. She never said no. Sometimes, as we held each other, a wave of love would sweep through me, and I would say something like "Wow! I just got hit by a wave of love! And I'm loving you so much!" To which she would reply, "Please! No big speeches!"

That's how it was on that Friday morning. I was up before 8:30, pulled back the drapes in the living room and the dining room, opened the kitchen blinds, marvelled at the blossoming cherry tree, and returned to bed for a cuddle. By 9:00 a.m. I was fully up, preparing Bella's breakfast—cooked cereal topped with sliced banana, kiwifruit, and assorted berries—while she remained in bed.

I don't remember why or when we developed this routine. Bella was a superb and innovative cook, and the kitchen was her domain. She called it her "laboratory." When she was at work there, it was best to stay out of her way. Which was fine by me. For years, I had been the often-surprised and

15

always delighted recipient of dishes I might otherwise expect only in the world's finest restaurants. But breakfast was not her thing. So in the interest of some semblance of reciprocity, breakfast had become *my* thing. Never very innovative. Usually just cereal; sometimes French toast.

Bella had discovered and cultivated her culinary skills under the tutelage of a French *Cordon Bleu* chef named Albert Charbon and a Swiss pastry chef named Max. Together they ran a delicatessen and patisserie called *Chez Charbon* in Toronto's Forest Hill Village neighbourhood. She had been hired to work at the sales counter because Monsieur Charbon had noted that she was not only gorgeous but immensely playful and socially outgoing. Monsieur Charbon himself liked to play, and they made a good team.

Bella was also an engaging storyteller who would often embellish the truth to increase the appeal of whatever story she was telling. It wouldn't have occurred to her that she was lying. Just gently sautéing the facts to make their recounting tastier. So she would tell of being "apprenticed" to Albert Charbon and becoming a "chef" in her own right. That wasn't true—though I never called her on it. Some embellishments are best simply accepted. And the truth is that, under Albert's tutelage, Bella did become an exceptional cook. She believed the adage that the way to a man's heart is through his stomach. I could have told her that it wasn't necessary. My heart was already in her keeping.

In any case, I had drifted into the role of breakfast chef. And then, as Bella more and more liked having breakfast in bed, also into the role of French waiter or *garçon de café*. She adored the French language—which she spoke far better than I did, despite my having lived in Canada for most of my first forty years—as well as French cuisine, French perfume, and anything else French. Had I myself been French, she might have thought she had already died and gone to heaven. As it was, she had to settle for my less-than-polished enactment of her *garçon de café*, complete with a white linen napkin folded over my forearm.

> *Bonjour, mon amour. Comment ça va? C'est une belle journée de printemps, et je t'aime. Ce matin, pour l'entrée, voici un verre de jus d'orange avec ton médication—les trois pilules.*

Breakfast began with a glass of orange juice and three prescription tablets—for low thyroid function, depression, and anxiety. I was not persuaded that Bella needed the antidepressant any longer, and was uneasy about the tranquillizer's addictive potential. But her doctor—Pippa Mackay at the Ilam Medical Centre, in whom we both had ample confidence—thought there was no point in risking the side effects often associated with withdrawal.

A few minutes later I returned with the main course: hot cereal served in a Corso de' Fiori soup bowl from a set of white Italian crockery ringed with blue goats. I always topped the cereal with a carefully arranged display of fruit. Usually sliced banana, gold kiwifruit, blueberries, and raspberries.

> *Et maintenant, mon amour, pour ton plaisir, le petit déjeuner—la céréale chaude et très délicieuse, avec la banane, le fruit de Kiwi, les myrtilles, et les framboises. Bon appétit!*

Bella in turn would respond with a French accent so perfect that the most sophisticated francophone would think she was Parisian. This was playtime. But then, virtually any time was playtime for Bella. Early in our relationship, she had said that she required only two things of the man she loved. He had to like poetry. And he had to make her laugh.

And so we played on that Friday morning when the cherry tree was in full bloom.

It must have been close to 9:30 when Bella passed through the dining room to return her Corso de' Fiori bowl to the kitchen sink. I had finished my own bowl of cereal and fruit and was still seated at the dining-room table, responding to e-mails that had arrived overnight. We didn't speak beyond my asking, "How're you doing, babe? Everything okay?" and her responding with, "Yes, I'm fine. Thank you for breakfast."

They were the last words I would hear her speak. No more Bella. No more playtime. No more of that oh-so-familiar, much-loved voice, still with just a hint of a Welsh accent across all these years. "Thank you for breakfast."

No! Thank *you*, my darling. Thank you so, so much for everything. For *everything*!

The next thing I heard, not more than three or four minutes later, was a sound I had never heard before and hope never to hear again. I later learned that it was the death rattle, which occurs when bronchial secretions accumulate in a dying person's throat and upper chest. "Darling, are you all right?" I called out as I rushed toward the bedroom. But there was no answer. Nothing but the death rattle.

And there she was. Slumped on the floor, in the doorway between the walk-in wardrobe and the bathroom. Topless, clad only in a pair of tight blue jeans. Her face was pallid, her lips were blue, and she was unconscious.

Later, I tried to reconstruct what must have happened in those last moments. She'd had sufficient strength, balance, and co-ordination to squeeze into those jeans. Then, because she was always modest, her next move would have been to reach for her bra. But her bra was nowhere at hand. So in a matter of seconds, she had fainted—perhaps holding to the doorpost as she slumped to the floor. Her heart had fallen apart. No more blood to the brain. Lights out!

I feel so sorry now that I couldn't truly *be* with Bella in those dying moments. I hadn't realized she was dying. That was impossible. Only *other* people die. I had been with her on three previous occasions when she had fainted. But each time, she had quickly regained consciousness. So this time, though it looked and sounded far more serious, that she was dying just didn't occur to me. I hadn't known that her noisy breathing was the *death rattle*. I mean, she *was* breathing. And she had been known sometimes to snore. So I eased her into a lying position, on her back, on the walk-in wardrobe's carpeted floor, and began calling to her: "Darling, don't leave me! Stay with me!" I think I was shouting what I'd heard movie characters shout in similar situations. I even wondered if I should slap her face, as I'd seen Doc Martin do on such occasions in the TV series by that name.

In retrospect, had I known and been able to accept that Bella was dying, I might have been able to truly *be there* for her—lovingly encouraging her to "let go" into the Light, as recommended by *The Tibetan Book of the Dead*° and seemingly confirmed by those who've had a near-death experience.°

Many years previously, Bella and I had attended a weekend workshop conducted by an esteemed Lama in the Karma Kagyu school of Tibetan

Buddhism. Ole Nydahl and his wife, Hannah, had cofounded the Diamond Way in 1972 and had since been travelling the world teaching their version of Vajrayana meditation. Why Bella and I chose to go escapes me now. Neither of us were much into Buddhism and, had we known that the weekend would consist in the endless repetition of what we assumed were Tibetan prayers, in a language we couldn't understand, we would almost certainly not have gone. But we were assured by Lama Ole that our chanting would open in each of us an inner channel through which, at the moment of our death, our spirit could easily exit through the top of our head, straight into the bosom of the Buddha. At the end of the workshop, the Lama carefully inspected each participant's scalp, identified a telltale drop of blood, and declared that the channel had indeed been opened.

Bella and I were less than impressed. But perhaps now, as my beloved lay dying on the floor of the walk-in wardrobe, she was indeed making such an exit. And if so, perhaps she was still in some sense *present*, in the way reported by those who have undergone a near-death experience. And if that were so, maybe I could have been there with her. Supporting her. Maybe even *celebrating* her release. Perhaps in those dying moments, I could have sung to her what Rashani Réa sang to her father as he lay dying:

> Cross over now, beloved one,
> to the shore where new life awaits you.
> Cross over now, beloved one,
> to the shore from whence you came.
> There is only love and forgiveness now
> and gratitude for all you've given,
> there is only love and forgiveness now
> and gratitude for all you've given.°

Or this song, also by Réa, based on a poem written by Thích Nhất Hạnh, the revered Vietnamese Buddhist monk and peace activist, who suggested that we sing it as a kind of lullaby to those who are dying. The words are derived from the *Sutta Pitaka*—a Buddhist scripture containing teachings attributed to the Buddha or his close disciples.

These eyes are not you,
you are not caught in these eyes.
You are life without boundaries.
You have never been born,
and you have never died.
Look at the ocean and sky filled with stars:
manifestations of your wondrous mind.
Since before time you have been free.
Birth and death are only doors
through which we pass,
sacred thresholds on our journey.
Birth and death are a hide-and-seek game.
So laugh with me, hold my hand,
let us say goodbye.
Say goodbye to meet soon again.
We meet today, we will meet tomorrow,
we shall meet at the source every moment.
We meet each other in all forms of life.°

Had I been able to sing something like that to Bella, her death rattle might have been interrupted by a laugh. The same signature laughter that had punctuated most of her days. And such laughter might have been the *right* response. The unimaginably perfect response to all that was unfolding. Which, when viewed with ordinary earthbound eyes, seemed only a disaster.

If only I could have seen with both sets of eyes—the inner as well as the outer! If only I could have wept and laughed at the same time! But that was quite impossible. I was in a rising panic, thinking mostly of myself. No, *not* thinking. Just *reacting* from a place of chronic self-interest. Calling to Bella, "Stay with me, darling! Please don't leave me! *Please* don't leave me!" And rushing to push the Call button on the bedroom wall.

Through a wall-mounted speaker, a voice—I think with an Australian accent—responded. It asked what help was needed. And then, within seconds, rang me on the cordless landline so that we could stay in touch while I cradled Bella's head in my lap. The voice said that an ambulance would be there soon.

I had little sense of time. But it couldn't have been more than five minutes before Brian and Jeanette arrived. Brian is the manager of our retirement village, and Jeanette is the resident liaison person. They, as well as the Aussie voice from the wall, are immediately alerted whenever a Call button is pushed. And they were wonderful! Jeanette found something with which to cover Bella's topless body. And then she took my place, cradling Bella's head, while I went to guide the arriving ambulance to our villa. I don't know why I did that. Brian would have done that. I could have stayed with Bella. But I didn't. At least I don't think I did. Everything was such a blur. I do know that within another few minutes, the ambulance arrived.

Paramedics shifted Bella from the walk-in wardrobe to the master bedroom. One of them immediately began CPR. Two others prepared defibrillator paddles. I couldn't watch. I returned to the living room.

It is said that there are no atheists in foxholes. I have never considered myself an atheist. But neither am I comfortable with the usual concept of God. Yet now, here I was, standing in the living room, my hands clasped before my face, lost in silent prayer. "Please, God, please be with Bella. Holy angels, surround her with your love and care. And please, please restore her to life and health." Over and over and over. "Please, God, please be with my sweet darling. Please don't let her die."

I'm not sure who else was in the room with me. Jeanette, I think, was nearby, having left Bella in the paramedics' care. And at some point, though I was unaware of their arrival, two police officers appeared on the scene. It didn't occur to me to wonder what possible reason *they* might have for being there. Mostly I was aware only of Brian's arm around my shoulder. He is a warm and supportive man. Available 24/7 to the residents of our retirement village. Thank you, Brian. A born-again Christian, he briefly offered up an audible prayer of his own, asking Jesus to heal whatever was afflicting Bella. I was glad his prayer was brief. Praying to Jesus is not my thing. I wanted to be alone, in the silence, with what I think of as the Beloved Mystery: my own version of divinity—which now, in my distress, had morphed into the Heavenly Father of my childhood. "Please, God, dear God, please be with Bella. Please don't let her die. But if she *is* dying, then please be with her. Hold her in your embrace, and keep her always in your love and care."

My sophisticated and skeptical friends would decry such prayer as foolishness. But I make no apology. For me, it works. It's a way of surfacing and focusing on what I most deeply desire, and aligning this as best I can with what I think is good and true and beautiful. Often it's an overflowing of gratitude. Or wonder. Sometimes it's a faltering attempt to surrender, to *let go* into the Mystery. And sometimes it's an anguished cry from the depths of my fear and helplessness.

So it was on that Friday morning. On that Friday morning, it would have been impossible for me *not* to pray.

"I'm sorry, but we had to let her go." In the infinite wisdom of the universe, many prayers go unanswered. Or do not receive the answer we want. "I'm sorry, but we had to let her go." I remember the words distinctly. They were spoken gently, kindly by one of the paramedics. I can still hear his voice. "We restarted her heart repeatedly," he said, "but each time it abruptly stopped again. Finally we had to let her go. I'm so sorry. Would you like us to place her body on the bed until the coroner arrives?"

"Yes, please."

No tears. No going weak at the knees. Just a stunned emptiness. A kind of blankness. And a courteous "Yes, please." And "Thank you for all that you have done."

I don't recall the paramedics leaving. Or Jeanette. Or Brian. I was sitting at the dining-room table with a police officer, answering his questions about Bella and what had happened. When he had finished and written it all down, I seem to recall signing something. Was this what TV detective dramas call "making a statement"? And then he insisted on taking with him whatever remained of Bella's medications. How bizarre! Did he think there was something suspicious about her death? I didn't think to ask. I was functioning on automatic. Like a robot. Perhaps even glad to have someone there with me while Bella lay dead in the next room. Only in retrospect did I wonder why the police were there at all. Or understand why the coroner needed to be involved. I later learned that New Zealand law requires an autopsy to determine the precise cause and manner of any sudden and unexpected death.

There are times when time itself seems to stop or stand still. When what is happening is so overwhelming that one cannot be anywhere other than *in* each moment. Only now, looking back on all that took place in those moments, can I guesstimate the time frame. I discovered Bella unconscious on the floor around 9:30 a.m. Attempts to resuscitate her must have stopped by 10:00. Everyone, including the police officer, had gone within the next half-hour. Leaving Bella and me alone together for perhaps another thirty minutes before the coroner arrived.

It was during this time—when I was alone with Bella—that my heart broke open. Kneeling beside the bed, holding her now-cold hand, talking to her, calling to her. "Sweet darling! My beloved!" She with whom I had playfully conversed in French as I served her breakfast in bed a little more than an hour earlier. And now she was gone.

I remember feeling a rush of anger, dismay, and disbelief. I simply could not compute that this oh-so-beautiful, vivacious, playful, creative, loving, forgiving being, who had shared this life with me for fifty years, who had brought such joy to so many people, who had learned so much through all that she had suffered and over all these years accumulated a wisdom that was uniquely Bella's—that all this could simply be annihilated in an instant. But that's how it was. Or so it seemed. All that she was, all that she had become over the course of a lifetime, all that she yet might be, would never be again. Here one instant, gone the next!

And if that's how it is, I thought, *then I am* seriously *pissed off. If that's how it is, then this life is nothing but a very bad cosmic joke. If that's how it is, then Sophocles had it right when, 2500 years ago, he wrote, "To never have been born may be the greatest boon of all."*⁰

I don't know how long I railed against the absurdity of it all. But, as best I recall, it wasn't long. For, as I knelt beside the bed, my dismay was swallowed up in a tidal wave of love. Nothing less than a tsunami of love poured through my broken heart. It was a love beyond anything I had ever known. A love so immense that I knew it wasn't *my* love but a love that fills the universe. A love at the heart of the universe. Of which my own expressions of love are a meagre trickle. But now, somehow, this breaking of my heart had opened the floodgates and allowed a previously dammed-up ocean of love to engulf me. Together, Bella and I were drowning in an ocean of love. In fact, *that's what we are. That's what we* all *are.* We are individual expressions of that love. *We are waves on an ocean of love.*

I wasn't *thinking* this. I *knew* it. It was as real as anything I have ever experienced. More than that, it was absolutely clear to me that our purpose in this life is to be, in our unique way, a free-flowing expression of that love. And that requires an open heart.

I suspect that all of us, if we have any powers of self-observation, know the difference between a closed and an open heart. Most of the time, perhaps of necessity, in the interests of preserving life and limb and of safely navigating this world, or simply maintaining the boundaries of my individuality, my heart remains more or less closed. A kind of toughness, a certain defensiveness, a somewhat anxious readiness to look out for Number One resides in the vicinity of my heart. And then there are times when I feel deeply touched by something quite beyond myself. When something moves me inwardly. The roar of ocean surf. A tiny flower blooming in some unlikely crevice. The plight of a war-ravaged refugee. Then my heart softens and opens a little. Then I feel more lovingly connected to my world, more available, more open to love and be loved. And always more vulnerable. "To love," as C.S. Lewis wrote, "is to be vulnerable."°

But what happened on that Friday morning, as I knelt beside Bella's lifeless body, was beyond, beyond, beyond anything I had ever experienced. Total brokenness. Total openness. Total vulnerability. Total love. Only recently did I come across words that come close to expressing what happened in those moments. "My heart has become an ocean," said Sufi mystic Pir Vilayat Inayat Khan, "since Thou hast poured Thy love into it."°

That's how it was on that Friday morning when time stood still. My heart became an ocean of love. And with that love came the stark awareness of how meagre had been my own expression of that love. I had loved Bella hugely over all these years. But now, as this tidal wave of love swept through me, I understood, I saw clearly, not as through a glass darkly but face to face, that even my most free-flowing love had been constricted, constrained, tainted by all my self-interest and ego-pretensions. It had passed through the reducing valve of my ego and emerged as a mere trickle from this ocean of love in which we have our being, to which we belong, and from which we can never truly be separate.

The arrival of the men from the coroner's office put me back on automatic again. Back into zombie mode. I watched as they carried Bella's body out the front door on a stretcher and placed her in the back of a black station wagon.

I watched as they drove away. Then, in an almost perfunctory manner, I made the necessary phone calls. First to Bella's daughter, Shelley, and then to her son, Tony. "Your mom died this morning." Then to each of my sons—Mark, Bruce, and Scott. Mark lives near Toronto, Bruce in Atlanta, and Scott in Sydney. Apart from Scott's saying that he'd come as soon as possible, I don't remember what the others said.

Then I did what I did on most mornings. I walked fifteen minutes down Roydvale Avenue, past the elementary school and day-care centre, to the coffee shop at Untouched World. Since moving to the retirement village three years earlier, Bella and I had taken this walk almost daily together. Always hand in hand. The coffee is great, the walk there and back gave us some exercise, and the shop's staff—especially Alan and Sue—adored Bella.

I hadn't known that memories can be so tactile. But as I walked, I could *feel* Bella's hand in mine. And my tears flowed freely now as I spoke to her. Quietly, but audibly. "Sweet darling." (That's almost always what I called her. If ever I called her "Bella," she'd think I was annoyed with her.) "Sweet darling. I love you so much. Please know how much I love you."

And when friends at Untouched World asked how Bella was, I said, "Bella died this morning."

～ THREE ～

"IN THE MIDST OF LIFE
WE ARE IN DEATH"

"I'm sorry, but we had to let her go."

Those words were as close to "pronounced dead" as anything I heard on the morning Bella died. Declared by one of the paramedics who staff the New Zealand ambulance service. I don't doubt their competence and am immensely grateful for the life-saving help they gave Bella on two previous occasions. But I was surprised that no more formal pronouncement was needed. I had presumed, based on news reports and TV dramas, that we need to be pronounced dead and the time of our death specified by a recognized medical professional. As when an accident victim is "pronounced dead on arrival" at the hospital. Or when, according to the *Warren Commission Report*, "At 1 p.m., after all heart activity ceased and the Last Rites were administered by a priest, President Kennedy was pronounced dead."° Perhaps it's only presidents and folk in TV dramas who are pronounced dead.

It's another of those strange expressions. "I pronounce you dead." What warrants such a pronouncement? "I now pronounce you husband and wife." A good friend, authorized to utter those words, had declared Bella and me to be married. A Toronto court had previously decreed that Carol and I were divorced. But no one pronounced me "alive" when I was born, or Bella "dead" when she died. She was later *certified* as dead, but this was dated six days after the paramedics "had to let her go," three days after her body had been dissected in an autopsy, two days after her remains had been cremated, and one day after family and friends had gathered to say goodbye. By which time no one could deny that she was well and truly dead.

Nor was it certified precisely *when* she died, other than at some time on October 16, 2015. With advances in Resuscitation Medicine, it can be difficult to identify the precise moment when someone dies. But at some unspecified moment, Bella suffered "cardiac death": that is, her heart stopped beating and could not be restarted. Another four months would pass, however, before the Coroner issued his decision "not to open an inquiry in respect of the death of Bella Dickinson."

"I have considered all available information," he wrote in his report, "and am satisfied that this person died as a result of natural causes." He went on to identify the *direct cause* of death as "haemopericardium and cardiac tamponade," the *antecedent cause* as "ruptured recent acute myocardial infarction," and the *underlying condition* as "coronary artery atherosclerosis." Freely translated, this means that the chambers of Bella's heart had been compressed by a sudden flooding of the pericardial sac with blood, caused by a dramatic rupture of her heart's left ventricular wall, caused by damage done by a silent heart attack anywhere from one day to three weeks earlier when a blood clot blocked the flow of blood to a portion of her heart, caused in turn by a gradual build-up of plaque in her coronary arteries. Thankfully, this catastrophic failure of her heart resulted in an almost immediate loss of consciousness and rapid cardiac death.

But I can't help wondering: when did Bella *begin* to die? Clearly, it's not as simple as "one moment you're alive and the next you're dead." Dying seems to be a *process* in which a *cause* is preceded by an *antecedent cause* created by some *underlying condition*. But when does the process begin? Studies of the *aging process* are very much in vogue, but perhaps that's just the *dying process* by another name.

Beyond a certain age, we all begin our return to the earth. Tits, ass, and earlobes sag—victims of earth's gravitational pull. My once-proud height of more than six feet tall has fallen to little more than five-foot-ten. At some point, damaged hair cells in the inner ear lead to a loss in hearing. In our forties, diminishing collagen renders our skin less elastic, blood pressure increases, and visceral fat begins to build around our heart. A decade earlier, in our thirties, cellular replication and repair had begun to slow and, as early as our twenties, our arteries had already begun to stiffen. In fact, you might say that we begin aging before we are born, when little defects start occurring in how our cells reproduce. Can the processes of living and dying be so intertwined as to be virtually inseparable?

Don Juan Matus, the Yaqui Indian shaman whom Carlos Castaneda, in *The Teachings of Don Juan*, claimed as his mentor, taught that, in each moment, "death is sitting next to you on the same mat."° That had made an impression on me. As had a verse from the Order for the Burial of the Dead, in the Book of Common Prayer used in Anglican and Episcopal churches: "In the midst of life we are in death."°

So when did Bella begin to die?

On the morning of the day before she died, I had persuaded her to go for a walk with me. If not all the way to the coffee shop, then as far as she felt comfortable in going. She had not fully recovered from a life-threatening illness she'd suffered fifteen months earlier, and I would often urge her to get at least a little exercise. On this occasion, she reluctantly agreed. It was a beautiful spring day. But we didn't get past the primary school, only halfway to the coffee shop, before she wanted to return home. It would be the last time we walked together hand in hand.

That afternoon, we were sitting together in our living room. I don't recall what I was doing. Probably reading. Bella was playing Scrabble by herself. We sometimes played together, but she loved the challenge of making words from the randomly selected tiles and would often do so by herself. That's what she had been doing a few years earlier when, just as she placed the word SHAKE on the Scrabble board, a massive earthquake rocked our house and destroyed much of Christchurch. Whether her account of that was true, slightly embellished, or entirely apocryphal, I couldn't say. And now on this occasion, on the afternoon before she died, as she played Scrabble by herself, she said something no less earth-shaking. She said, almost casually, "I think I'm getting ready to go."

"*I think I'm getting ready to go.*" My God, woman, I thought, *do you know what you're saying? That's not a throwaway line.* Of course I didn't take her seriously. Only other people die. I don't know what I said in response. Probably something like "Yeah, right!" But she didn't elaborate, and I didn't ask what she meant. She seemed fine. Nothing was amiss. I just didn't take her seriously.

Now, in retrospect, and prompted by some guilt, I wonder: What was she experiencing? No one *casually* says, "I think I'm getting ready to go." Did she really *know*, by some uncanny intuition, that she was dying? As the Coroner's report later made clear, her heart muscle was in fact dying. But on that afternoon, there were no symptoms. She was in no evident distress. Yet *she seemed to know that she was dying.* She said, "I think I'm getting ready to go," and I didn't take her seriously. And if I *had* taken her seriously, what would we have done? Rushed to the hospital in an effort to arrest the dying process? That wouldn't have happened. Bella had had enough of hospitals.

I wonder too: What if I hadn't urged her to take that morning walk with me? She hadn't *wanted* to go. She said yes just to make me happy. Had that bit of exercise set the dying process in motion? I don't really think so. But I can't help wondering.

~

For more than a year before she died, Bella had not been well. She'd been hospitalized a few times and was determined never to go back. She'd rather die than return to hospital. Was this all part of the dying process?

Eighteen months earlier, on April 28, 2014, she had been diagnosed with acute pseudogout in her right knee. Some coincidences are nothing less than uncanny. April 28 was the date, in 1956, when Carol and I were married. It was the same date, in 1972, when Bella and I were married. And now, in 2014, this red-letter date may have marked the beginning of the end of her life.

There is nothing very serious about pseudogout, apart from the fact that it is painful. A form of degenerative arthritis that usually occurs in a knee, it is clearly related to aging. Bella's fingers were already arthritic. And now it was in her knee.

For several days, her knee had been so painful that she'd had trouble walking. But no diagnosis was made until late in the afternoon of April 28, in the office of our GP in Sumner. Twelve hours before we were to leave on an overseas trip to visit family and friends in North America and attend a grandson's wedding. Now, at the last minute, something needed to be done to reduce the inflammation and ease Bella's pain. That could be done in either of two ways—quickly, with a cortisone injection in her knee; or more gradually, by taking a non-steroidal anti-inflammatory drug (an NSAID).

Though cortisone injections are considered safe, our GP warned us that there were occasional side-effects and the possibility of infection, which, if they were to occur, would not be evident until we were already overseas. And overseas is not a good place to become ill from a pre-existing condition not covered by insurance. So we opted for an NSAID. The doctor wrote a prescription for 200 Naproxen tablets. He said that Bella could take up to eight per day as needed—always with a glass of water, preferably with food, and together with another drug designed to protect the stomach lining from possible damage caused by NSAIDs. Throughout our trip, Bella did as the doctor ordered—though she never took more than four Naproxen in a day. And it did no good at all. She continued to be crippled by the pain.

Despite which, we had a fabulous time. Bella was her usual vivacious self. We laughed and played regardless of the circumstance. Wheelchair assistance at every airport. Helping her to the loo on the long trans-Pacific flight. Watching life go by on a San Francisco street from the window of a hotel room that Bella was unable to leave. Limping through five days in New York City, where we had wanted to "do the town" one more time. Playing non-stop with Bruce and Angie on a two-day motor trip from Atlanta to Toronto, and back again—singing most of the way, including the entire soundtrack from *The Sound of Music*. Wrapping Bella in a plastic garbage bag en route to Mitch and Alicia's wedding, because the dress she had bought for the occasion kept dropping sequins wherever she went. And then lunch with a group of family and friends, being as *Yiddishe* as we who were *goyim* knew how to be, playing outlandishly at Caplansky's outlandish Jewish delicatessen on College Street in Toronto.

Thank you, my love. Thank you so much for being, despite your pain, so irrepressibly "you."

When we returned to Christchurch, on the afternoon of June 5, our first stop was the Ilam Medical Centre to register as new patients. Having recently moved to the retirement village, a forty-minute drive from our former GP, we needed a doctor closer to home. And we were eager to see what else might be done to ease the pain of Bella's pseudogout. It proved a timely decision.

At about 6:00 a.m. the following day, I was awakened by Bella's call for help. She had fallen, presumably fainted, on the floor of the walk-in wardrobe, on her way to or from the toilet. I was alarmed, but she insisted she was all right and there was no need to press the Call button. She had previously fainted on two recent occasions, for seemingly innocuous reasons, with no ill after-effects.

Five years earlier, while dining at a Toronto restaurant, she had suddenly passed out. Dropped like a stone and remained unconscious on the floor for several seconds. An ambulance took her to St. Michael's Hospital, where she was said to be dehydrated, given intravenous fluids, and discharged. Apparently none the worse for wear. Then, a year later, in March 2011, she again fainted—this time while standing with a few hundred others in a street-festival atmosphere in the centre of Sumner, awaiting the arrival of Prince William, who was touring what was left of Christchurch after the catastrophic earthquake a month earlier. She was helped to an ambulance, on hand for precisely this kind of situation, where a quick cardiogram and checks of her blood pressure and blood sugar revealed nothing amiss. The even better news was that, as we exited the back of the ambulance, she very nearly walked straight into the arms of the Prince himself. That made her day. Since her childhood in Wales, Bella had always been enamoured of British royalty.

So on this occasion, on the morning after our return from overseas, Bella had again fainted, quickly recovered, and assured me that she was all right. This time, however, I was determined to call her new GP, Pippa Mackay, just as soon as the Medical Centre opened in a couple of hours' time. Which is what I did. But no sooner had I made the call than I heard Bella fall again. She had fallen off the toilet, momentarily passed out, and was sitting in her own mess on the bathroom floor. Now we were both alarmed. I cleaned her up as best I could, helped her dress, and drove the few blocks to the Medical Centre. Pippa asked what had happened, conducted relevant tests, and sent an urgent blood sample to the lab. Having never previously seen Bella as a patient, she was unsure what to make of the situation—until I said, "The stools in which Bella was lying on the bathroom floor looked black. Could she be bleeding internally?" No more needed to be said. As Bella was being lifted into an ambulance, the results of her blood test came through. "Her haemoglobin count is seriously low," Pippa said, "but it's not life-threatening. She should be all right."

The next six days in hospital were difficult but encouraging. Blood transfusions maintained Bella's red blood count, and a second gastroscopy found the source of the bleed: a Dieulafoy's lesion with spurting bleeding from one of the major arteries feeding her stomach, caused by extended use of the anti-inflammatory medication. Two tiny titanium haemostatic clips were successfully placed. The bleeding stopped. And Bella returned home on June 12.

Then three days later, what had been a bad dream became a nightmare. We had been together throughout the day. Bella had not indicated that she was feeling weak or ill. And I hadn't noticed that she was becoming ever paler. But when Joy Holdsworth, a friend and neighbour, came by just before dinnertime with some food she had prepared for us, she took one look at Bella and said, "Press the Call button *now!*" Joy, a retired nurse, had noticed at once that Bella was dangerously pale. Within minutes, paramedics were on the scene. and Bella was again rushed to hospital. Only after she had been stabilized with blood transfusions did one of the nurses say to me: "I hadn't known it was possible to survive with a haemoglobin count that low."

For the next several days, the nightmare only worsened. Two more attempts to staunch the bleeding with haemostatic clips failed. Bella was now receiving multiple blood transfusions and was projectile vomiting the accumulations of blood in her stomach. The decision was made to insert a plug into the artery that was bleeding. Doing so would effectively kill the artery as well as the spleen that it was feeding, but two other major arteries would suffice to keep the stomach alive. This procedure, known as a coil embolization, also failed, leaving Bella in enormous distress and under constant surveillance in Intensive Care. Her surgeon then proposed the only remaining option—to open her abdomen surgically and stitch up the lesion from inside.

We were together when he told us the risks and asked for Bella's signature to authorize the surgery. Her chances of surviving it, he said, were 50:50. And it was possible that he might have to remove all or part of her stomach, leaving only the small intestine to digest what small amounts of food she would be able to eat. I'm not sure how much of this Bella was able to understand, but she signed on the dotted line.

We had only a few minutes alone together before they took her to the operating theatre. She was scarcely able to speak. I told her how much I loved her and how hugely grateful I was for all her love. I kissed her, asked her to please come back to me, and, choked with tears, managed to sing the chorus of "We'll Meet Again," made famous by Vera Lynn during World War II.° I know that sounds melodramatic. But songs just have a way of coming to my mind. And from her childhood, during the war years in Britain, Bella had always liked Vera Lynn.

She was in surgery and then in recovery for most of the day. I went straight to the hospital chapel, where on other days I had often spent time between visiting hours. There was never anyone else there, and these times alone, enveloped in the Mystery, gave me comfort and strength. It was here, gazing at a simple wooden cross on the wall behind the altar, that I saw clearly, as if for the first time, that suffering and love stand together at the very heart of life. And just a few steps from the chapel, the hospital café served surprisingly good coffee and superb chocolate cake. Together, they provided the sustenance I needed.

When I was finally able to see Bella, who was still in Intensive Care, her surgeon was there as well. He said it had been "touch and go." But the surgery had been successful, the bleeding had been stopped, and nothing of Bella's stomach had needed to be removed. Even her spleen, which should have been killed by the coil embolization, was still functioning. What can one say at such a time except "Thank you"?

It would be another ten days before Bella could be transferred to another hospital for rehabilitation, and a further ten days before she was permitted to return home. It had been five weeks since her first admission. Only in retrospect do I recognize what a toll all this took on her.

The ensuing fifteen months were an emotional rollercoaster of alternating hope and dismay. And she never recovered her *joie de vivre*.

Bella had often said how fortunate she was to know, with certainty, what her purpose was in life. And how simple it was to fulfil. All she had to do was *sparkle*. And throughout her life she had done it beautifully, bringing joy to virtually everyone she met. But now she could no longer sparkle. Was this the beginning of the end?

Perhaps when we can no longer do what is ours to do—when we have played our part, delivered our lines, and performed our role in the drama—it may be time then to make our exit. "For everything there is a season," says the Bible: "a time to be born, and a time to die."° "All the world's a stage," wrote the Bard, "And all the men and women merely players; / They have their exits and their entrances."° I like to think that Bella choreographed her exit perfectly. Throughout the changing scenes of her life drama, she had sparkled. She had done what was hers to do. And now her sparkling days were over. Destiny fulfilled! "I think I'm getting ready to go."

~

Two months after Bella died, I spent time with Scott and Natsuko in Australia. We stayed for three nights, near Coffs Harbour, at an Airbnb rental spectacularly situated in the Australian bush. A spacious living room with floor-to-ceiling windows gave the impression of being *in* the bush. Early each morning I would sit there by myself, listening to the dawn chorus of a thousand birds—finches, lorikeets, cuckoos, thornbills—filling the treetops, doing whatever it is birds do. With them, the mating calls of millions of cicadas, each one only hours from its death, rose and fell like waves sweeping through the bush with a kind of lazy urgency. Meanwhile, here and there, camouflaged against the undergrowth, roos and wallabies could sometimes be seen grazing in the shade.

It was patently clear to me that all of nature is this constant interplay of life and death. All these creatures being born, living out their lives and dying, in succeeding generations long or short. It could not be otherwise. Life and death are part of the same fabric. Woven together so closely as to interpenetrate each other. The warp and weft of an indivisible tapestry. That's just how it is. *And we are part of it.*

How could I ever have forgotten this? How could I be so mistaken as to think of death as an enemy? What could possibly be my objection when it's all so perfect? "In the midst of life we are in death." YES! *And it's all okay!*

I want so much not to forget what in those moments I saw to be true! How is it that we manage to distance ourselves from this life-and-death drama? Retreating into our high-tech urban cocoons where scarcely a bird is heard. Chasing some non-existent security. There to disguise with nips and tucks and anti-aging potions the natural trajectory of life. Pretending for as long as possible that death is what happens to other people.

It doesn't have to be that way. For millennia, our hunter–gatherer forebears felt a deep connection with the natural world. A chorus of praise rose up spontaneously in response to their intimations of transcendence. And they could say with a deep honesty as they greeted each day, "Today is a good day to die."⁰

~ FOUR ~
"IS THAT YOU, DARLING?"

What was clear to me as I contemplated the Australian bush two months after Bella died was not at all clear to me in the hours and days immediately following her death. Far from recognizing the blessed necessity of death-in-the-midst-of-life, I was appalled by what seemed the absurdity of it all. One minute, here. Lovingly playful. The next minute, gone. Our partnership, our deepening love, had not come easy. Fifty years of joyful, painful learning to love. And now it was over. Everything that Bella was, seemingly extinguished. In an instant. It was beyond my comprehension. Light-years removed from anything I could accept.

Since time immemorial, people in every culture have chosen to believe that their loved ones live on in some other realm after death. Like them, I desperately needed to believe that now. That Bella was still present. That she had not been annihilated, that her light had not been extinguished. People would later say, "Bella lives on in our memories." And I would think, *Memories be damned! It's Bella that I want! Memories are just painful reminders of what's been lost. What good is all this love if she's not here to share it?* I needed *Bella.* I needed our *relationship.* I needed to feel that she could *hear* me as I called out over and over, "Darling, darling. My sweet love. Sweet darling. I love you so much." But of course I was talking to a corpse. It seemed the cruellest of jokes. And I was angry. Deeply cynical. In paroxysms of grief.

And at the same time—or almost at the same time, in a kind of simultaneous alternation—I was engulfed in a tsunami of love. I don't know how that's possible. How can one be in such anguish, erupting into wrathful protest, and be engulfed by love at the same time? But that was my experience. Huge suffering, flashes of ice-cold anger, and an ocean of love!

Beyond anything I had previously known. They all came together on the morning Bella died. And together they split my heart wide open.

Sometimes the pain is too much and issues not in angry protest but in abject denial. Fifty years ago, in her book *On Death and Dying*, Elisabeth Kübler-Ross identified anger and denial as early stages in the grief process.° But they don't occur in any tidy linear progression. Grief is too messy for that.

When her mother died in 1953, denial was Bella's overwhelming first response. She hadn't known her father. He had died when Bella was just thirteen months old. And a half-brother from her father's previous marriage, much older than Bella, had moved out of the family home when she was still young. So Bella grew up virtually as an only child, closely bonded with her mother. And then, during her final year of high school, she watched her mother die a painful death from cancer.

She was alone at home on the morning her mother died. There were few telephones in Wales then, so the hospital sent someone with the news. To which Bella replied, "Thank you." A watchful neighbour called out from across the street, "How's your mother this morning?" Bella answered, "She's fine, thank you." Then she went inside, locked the door, and refused to see or speak to anyone for days. She didn't attend the funeral. She didn't sit *shivah*, as Jewish custom requires of first-degree relatives during a weeklong period of mourning. She had no idea how, over the ensuing weeks, the large family home and its furnishings were sold. She was numb with grief. Felt nothing. So, with scarcely a backward glance, she packed a bag, moved to Swansea thirty miles away, and promptly married Ronnie—a man five years older than she was, to whom she'd become engaged just a few months earlier, while her mother lay dying. Bella was only eighteen. *That's what is known as "denial."*

Was I in denial on the morning Bella died? Perhaps. Though her all-too-dead body was only too real, I could not accept that she was gone. But *anger?* Absolutely! Directed at whatever gods may be, in protest at the incomprehensible finality of what had happened. An anger strangely mixed with love. Anger tossed about like flotsam, the wreckage of my heart, visible one minute and gone the next behind another wave on an ocean of love.

How else can I describe it? This anger and this being engulfed by love were like a counterpoint. A *both–and*. Forces moving simultaneously in opposite directions in the region of my heart. The anger felt like a hardening of my heart. A toughening of myself against the outrage of what had happened. The tsunami of love moved in the opposite direction, sweeping everything before it. Opening me. It was not *my* love. It was *Love-from-the-Source*. It was not so much a *feeling* as *the all-pervasive way things are*. Despite my anger, I had become a conduit of a Love that seemed the very Essence of who I am. And who you are. And who we all are. *I am IN LOVE! We are all IN LOVE.* Even while we are angrily protesting the way things are.

Later, as I reflected on what had so overwhelmed me as I knelt beside Bella's body, waiting for the Coroner, it seemed an answer to a Baha'i prayer that I had learned long ago and adapted for my own use: "Make of me a hollow reed from which the pith of self has been blown, that I may be an open channel of Thy love." I hadn't known that the prayer could be answered only in the breaking of my heart.

I discovered too that I couldn't stay there. I could not remain immersed in this openhearted torrent of love. It seemed out of place in a world where things need to get done. And things in my world needed to get done. Contacting family and friends. Making arrangements with a funeral home. Planning a memorial service. So the tsunami of love abated. My heart closed again. And my anger easily resurfaced whenever it found cause.

It smouldered just beneath the surface throughout my meeting with the funeral director on that Friday afternoon. He was, in my books, inappropriately businesslike. Cool. Matter-of-fact. No empathy. Perhaps he was less than happy on discovering that I abhorred polished mahogany coffins, shiny black hearses, and other costly accoutrements associated with what some call "a dignified farewell." Or perhaps he had simply learned from experience how to prevent people from having emotional meltdowns in his office.

I was more volubly angry that evening when, about to get into my now-empty bed, I stubbed my toe, and broke it, against a leg of the bed. Howls of pain! Howls of fury! Did my psychic pain need this physical expression? Did I create this moment as an excuse to vent my rage?

The most persistent, if less evident, anger was generated simply by the fact of Bella's absence and the certainty that she would not return. She was not on vacation. This was not a temporary separation. She was *gone*. And there was nothing to suggest that she lived on in any other realm—unlike my mother, who had "dropped in on me" shortly after she died in 1982.

Bella and I had emigrated to New Zealand the previous year and could not be with my mother when she died. But some thirty-six hours after her death, I felt her presence. I remember precisely where I was: standing in the living room of our house in Okato. It was midmorning. And suddenly she was there. For just a few seconds. Nothing visible, but a powerful presence nonetheless. She was ageless. Neither young nor old. And immensely stronger than I had ever known her to be in this life. I had no doubt that I had glimpsed her soul—and that she had come to let me know that all was well.

So now, where was Bella? Why could I not feel her presence in the same way? Granted, I'd had no such "visitation" when my father died in 1999, two days after his hundredth birthday. Or when my older brother, Ron, died in 2005. Maybe I had only *imagined* my mother's presence. No matter how vivid the experience, I am quite capable of doubting it. Indeed, if you had asked me before Bella died, "Do you believe that consciousness survives our physical death?" I would have said that I simply don't know, while acknowledging that I was open to being happily surprised. But now, despite the question being fundamentally unanswerable, I could no longer be so blasé in my agnosticism. I *wanted* to believe that Bella, and all that she was, had not been annihilated. But there was no evidence to suggest otherwise. She was gone. The heavens were silent. And I was angry.

If there was anything during those first few days for which I could be grateful, it was the prompt arrival of Scott from Sydney, and Natsuko a few days later. They stood with me through all that needed to be done and eased the pain of facing my new reality alone. Then, on Sunday morning, I was supported by a group of friends who have been meeting once a month for more than twenty years in what is known as the Sunday Gathering. But most surprising was the thoughtful consideration of the staff from the Coroner's Office. If we wished, they said, we could see Bella one last time: on Sunday afternoon, at the hospital morgue.

Which is what we did. Scott and I were taken to a small but warmly lit room where Bella's body was laid out, under blankets, on a single bed. Though we were assured that we could spend as much time with her as we wanted, we did not stay long. Her body was cold. And it was clear that Bella wasn't there. *There was no one at home.* Still, this was the body that, for so many years, I had loved and that I would never see again. I kissed her and said goodbye. Then we clipped a lock of her hair and left. I don't recall what I was feeling. There were tears, of course. But no anger. I was empty. Bereft. Cold inside. And immensely alone. Trying to come to terms with the incomprehensible reality that I would never see my sweet darling again.

But the next day—suddenly, surprisingly, wondrously—everything changed. It happened early Monday morning. Scott was still in bed. Natsuko had not yet arrived from Sydney. I was in the kitchen, gathering together what we might have for breakfast. I remember exactly where I was. Standing at the counter, facing the corner window. The cherry tree was very much in bloom. Then, just to my left and slightly above eye level, there was Bella. In an instant. Just as my mother had been years earlier. Not visible. But *there. Present.*

"Is that you? Is that you, darling?" I said softly, but audibly. There was no reply. But I *knew.*

Later, I thought: *Of course! How perfect! Where else would Bella make herself known but in the kitchen?* It was her domain. Her laboratory. Perhaps she just wanted me to know she would be with me in what to me was foreign territory.

I kept what had happened to myself. It was between Bella and me. Too precious to risk the ridicule of those who are certain that death is the end—who would have explained to me, in gently condescending terms, that this was of course a manifestation of my denial. So, like Mary, when she discovered she was the bearer of divinity, I kept all these things and pondered them in my heart.°

≈

The sense of Bella's presence recurred again and again over the ensuing days. Always unexpectedly. Unlike *memories,* which I can easily recall at will, this was not something I could conjure up. Her actual *presence* would suddenly surprise me. This is not, I am told, an uncommon experience. Many who have lost a close loved one report something similar. A presence so real they find it hard to dismiss as mere wishful thinking.

Knowing that Bella was there made things easier for me. That certainly was true during the memorial service. We had each, on a few occasions in recent years, envisioned how we'd like our memorial service to be arranged. So I knew what to do. The chapel chairs were placed in concentric circles, surrounding a small low table bearing the urn of ashes and two brass Sabbath candlesticks brought from Russia long ago by Bella's grandparents. We had agreed, too, since it seemed wrong to have the service conducted by some unknown rabbi, priest, or secular celebrant, that I would serve in that capacity. So, supported by Scott and Natsuko, and wearing a *yarmulke* and prayer shawl that were among Bella's family heirlooms, I began the service. I lit the candles and invoked the Hebrew blessing.

> *Baruch Atoh Adonai Eloheynu Melech Ha-Olam Ashe*
> *Kidshona B'mitzvosov V'trivonu L'hadlik Nayr Shell*
> *Zichron Yakar Beyla Yaffa bat Chana*

> Blessed art Thou, Lord God, King of the Universe, who
> has sanctified us with His command to kindle the lights
> in memory of dear Bella, daughter of Annie Jacobs

What followed was rich with music, readings, prayers, and tributes. Tributes sent by our sons and daughter who were unable to be with us, and expressed spontaneously by many who were present. Together they spoke of the joy and laughter, the depth and wisdom, that Bella had brought into their lives. An outpouring of love and gratitude for Bella's life and for all that she had meant to us.

When I concluded the service with the Hebrew benediction, it was an intensely personal prayer for Bella.

> The Lord bless you and keep you.
> The Lord make his face to shine upon you, and be
>   gracious to you.
> The Lord lift up His countenance upon you, and give
>   you peace.°

And then for all of us:

> O Lord, support us all the day long of this troublous
>   life,
> Until the shadows lengthen, and the evening comes,
>   and the busy world is hushed, and the fever of life
>   is over, and our work done.
> Then, of Thy tender mercy, grant us a safe lodging, a
>   holy rest, and peace at the last.°

Despite my intermittent tears, conducting the service had not been difficult. I was borne up on this ocean of love. Together we were honouring Bella. We had come together to express our love, not just for Bella but for each other. Grief and love are so closely intertwined. Grief opens our hearts to feel and express our love with a fullness that we seldom allow, or seldom are able to access, in the ordinary course of life. And I had no doubt that Bella was among us.

The next day, Scott and I took her ashes to where she had wished them scattered: in Hagley Park, near a tree planted by the Dalai Lama when he visited Christchurch in 1992. Bella and I had been among a small group with the Dalai Lama on that occasion, and she liked him very much. I had been uneasy at the prospect of seeing her ashes, of seeing all that remained of the body I had loved so much. Nor did I do so without tears. But scattering her ashes felt so right. Again I felt that we were honouring Bella. Letting her go in a place of great beauty, as she had wished. "Earth to earth, ashes to ashes, dust to dust."°

I take comfort from knowing that, in due course, my own ashes will be mingled with Bella's. I need so much to believe that I will one day be with her again. To think otherwise seems quite impossible. My emotional need is so much stronger than any rational assessment of the apparent reality. So I choose to believe that we will be together again. Until then, I'll keep the ship afloat as best I can. But it's so much more okay now for me to die. As if her passing on before me has made heaven more homelike to my heart.

~

On the following Monday, ten days after Bella died, I went again to the Dalai Lama's tree. Wanting to be with her. As I stood alone at the spot where we had scattered her ashes, covered now by a blanket of pine needles, I recalled the words spoken by an angel to Mary Magdalene when she visited Jesus' tomb on that first Easter morning: "Why do you seek the living among the dead? He is not here."°

Of course, I thought. *Bella is not here. Why do you seek the living among the dead?*

It was a beautiful spring morning, and it seemed as if Bella had dissolved into the One. The One to whom we all belong, in whom we have our being, and from whom we can never be separate. It was as if she was all around me. In the trees and flowers and blue sky. And at the same time, she felt very present to me—as if she had joined my guardian angels and was watching over me. Though part of the One, she remained a distinct point of consciousness or presence. But she was no longer the small earthly Bella. She was strong, steady as a rock, yet without personality. More like an angelic presence who would always be with me and continue to watch over me, with huge love, until I join her again in the Oneness of all things.

From the moment Bella died, and still to this day, at times and places when no one else can hear me, I find myself spontaneously speaking to her. Speaking her name aloud. Telling her how much I love her. And thanking her for loving me. I do this without regard to whether she might be able to hear me. It just seems a natural expression of my grief that I have no wish to restrain.

But now it occurred to me that perhaps this need not be a one-way street. If Bella really *is* present—if she is *ever-present*, albeit in some other dimension, in the One to whom we all belong—she might have something to say to me. So, on the morning after my visit to the Dalai Lama's tree, I began an early morning practice that I have come to call *deep listening*. I would sit, still my mind as I have done for years in meditation, and inwardly "listen" for whatever "message" might take shape in my mind. Sometimes I would sit for several minutes, aware of nothing but my breathing. At other times, often quickly, as I sought to open myself to whatever inner connection might be possible, a phrase would emerge in my mind and I would write it down. This would be followed by another phrase, and then another, in a phrase-by-phrase message that unfolded without my having any sense of where it was going. And always, the message was, to me at least, emotionally more powerful and imbued with a more intuitive sense of truth than anything that in my ordinary state of mind I could have created.

Are these messages actually from Bella? Or are they the product of my imagination? I don't pretend to know. But I suspect that the answer need not be *either–or*. Imagination may not simply be a fanciful view of things, adopted in this case for my comfort in the absence of hard evidence, but instead a means of reaching out to a transcendent Mystery that, by its very nature, is inaccessible to our ordinary mode of rational or sensible knowing. Whatever the case, these "messages from beyond" are shaped as Bella's response to my outpourings of grief and love. They are my intensely personal *conversations with Bella*.

Here is the first message. The opening words—"Hello, you!"—are an expression of deeply loving recognition that Bella and I would often speak to each other in moments of intimate connection.

Hello, you.

All is very well.
My transition was beautiful—very "Bella."
You need have nothing to fear.
I will not leave you—ever.
That is impossible. We are one.

Love is different here.
It doesn't ebb and flow; it's not a feeling; it just is.
I love you now with complete steadiness,
and will be with you always.
You need only "look up" and you will know that I am here.

Thank you for the memorial service.
It's important that you all find ways to express your love.

That's what earthly life' is for.
It's where' we' try to give' expression, in time' and space', to what is
eternally true'.

Enough! Ça suffit! Bonjour, mon amour!

This was the first of many "conversations" that assure me that the love story and the spiritual odyssey we shared are not over. Still inseparable. Still building on each other, like those baroque fugues. But transposed now into a higher key by the gift of a broken heart.

∽ FIVE ∽
NO SEPARATION

My conversations with Bella over the ensuing months carried one consistent and recurring message that brought comfort to my grief-stricken heart:

> There is no separation. We belong to the Whole—to an ocean of love that fills the universe, from which nothing, including death, can ever separate us. Our task is to be an open channel of that Love, here in this world of space and time.

That was my experience on the morning Bella died. The torrent of grief that swept through me was at the same time a tidal wave of love. I hadn't known there could be such love. A love that was orders of magnitude beyond anything I had previously experienced. And Bella and I were together *in* this love. Enveloped in this love. Engulfed by what seemed an ocean of love.

It was clear to me, not in thought or words but in my actual experience, that this vast, pervasive, all-inclusive Love is at the heart of the universe. It embraces everything. *My* love, *our* love, whether for our partners, our children, the world of nature, or that Beloved Mystery that some call God, is but a tiny expression—a tiny, all-too-flawed, down-here-on-the-ground manifestation—of a Love that fills the universe. And our task, our *raison d'être* in this life, is to open ourselves more and more to this Love. To know that we *are*, despite all our resistance and self-promotion, manifestations of this Love.

But words like these should never become an article of faith. Never something we *believe* rather than *know* and *live*. Our words only point to, but cannot capture, the reality we are trying to express. Please God, may I never be so seduced by my words that they cloud the reality of what I have experienced. The words taking shape in my conversations with Bella feel like a bulwark against that danger. They remind me of my lived experience. And bring me close again to what cannot be captured in words.

~

In some of these messages, I am addressed as "Meru"—the nickname Bella gave me years ago. She called me "Meru"; I called her "sweet darling." Terms of endearment uniquely ours.

The following messages speak of that Love to which we all belong and that is ours to express.

> My love for you is like a strong and steady beam of light that extends
>   to everyone.
> That's just how it is.
> My love for you overflows in a love that embraces everything.
> I am "at home" in a realm where we all belong and from which we
>   are never separate,
> which completely and always infuses and interpenetrates our mortal
>   life.
>
> But none of these words express the reality;
> the reality is beyond all such words.
> Think of me now as this strong and steady beam of light.
> Know that you are love, and that all is very well.

> What remains is love—love with a distinctive hint of Bella.
> Love is at the heart of everything;
> love is what holds everything together.
> You are an expression of that love;
> that is what and who you are.

Death does not change that.
The earthly form and personality dissolves (the loss of what you
*   grieve is real),*
but the love endures.
This is what surrounds you always, closer than your breathing.

I wish I could describe to you how it is—
beyond anything you can imagine.
But, for now, your life is in this world,
with all its fears and anxieties, sorrows and suffering—
the training ground, the testing ground
for your soul's development.

Continue the work of making these inner connections.
Practice being open and loving.
And in due course we will be together again.

I love you, Meru; I always will.
Rest assured that you are held by my love.
Nothing can ever separate you from the love of God that is in Bella.
Love is one; it is not fragmented;
our love is a unique expression of the love of God.

So feel that love; be in that love;
you yourself are a channel of that love.
Keep that channel clear of all self-interest or complaint or negativity
*   of any kind,*
and the love we share will flow strong and free.

∿

As a kind of corollary to this "love-at-the-heart-of-the-universe" theme, other messages emphasized the theme of "no separation." Although we are distinct individuals, we are inseparably one in this ocean of love. That too was my experience on the morning Bella died. In that tsunami of grief, she and I were more inseparably one than I could either fully comprehend or easily express. The words taking shape in these messages, however, gave voice to this in a straightforward way.

> There is no separation.
> I am with you always—
> as close to you as the air you breathe.
>
> There is no distance between us.
> We are inseparably linked—
> part of the Whole now and in eternity.
> But the Whole to which we belong
> is beyond anything our earthly mind can conceive of or imagine.
>
> Please know, and trust, my darling,
> that I am always with you and that all is well.

———————————

> What can I say more than I have said?
> There is no separation; we are one.
> I know that is hard for your mind to grasp,
> but that's how it is.
>
> The challenge, the burden in being human
> is to be the distinct individual you are
> while remembering that you are one with the Whole—
> remembering that inner connection that cannot be broken.
>
> This is the "ocean of love" in which you have your being—
> in which all things have their being and are never separate.

———————————

> It's hard for you to believe
> because you see everything in terms of distance
> and it often seems to you that I am far away.

In truth, there' is no distance'—only Presence'.
I am neither far away nor close' at hand; I am simply present.
Present where? There' is no "where."
It's hard to believe' because' it's impossible' to imagine'.
Your mind tries to imagine' and wants to believe;
but only your heart knows.

So "Hello," my love'. Hello! Hello! I love' you always.
Know that you are' held in eternal love'
and that nothing can ever separate' us.
Take' care; darling.
Live' well. Love' freely.

∼

From the time we are born into this life as separate beings, it is essential that we grow in independence and in our ability to manage our life as responsible agents. I have always assumed that this is how it is and this is who I am. A separate self. A responsible agent. For whom a healthy sense of separation is vital. Fritz Perls, the founder of Gestalt Therapy, expressed this idea in what he called "the Gestalt prayer":

> I do my thing, and you do your thing.
> I am not in this world to live up to your expectations
> And you are not in this world to live up to mine.
> You are you and I am I,
> And if by chance we find each other, it's beautiful.
> If not, it can't be helped.°

That's just how it is, I thought. You and I are separate individuals. And if by chance we find each other, as Bella and I did, it's beautiful. Or *mostly* beautiful. We reach out across the gap between us to connect as best we can. And when in death we are finally parted, that too is just the way it is. The ultimate separation. The last goodbye.

Except that on the morning Bella died, that was *not* the way it was. In those moments, and in other blissful moments since, my experience has been that just the opposite is true. *There is no separation. We are inseparably one in an ocean of love.* Nor is death the irrevocable separation that we fear, but the portal to a more profound experience of our essential oneness in an all-embracing Whole. Or so it seemed on the morning Bella died.

It is possible of course that my experience of *no separation,* however blissful, is nothing but a strange anomaly. A comforting denial of a reality too painful to confront. Occasioned perhaps by unusual neural activity prompted by the overwhelming intensity of emotion that accompanies a broken heart. God knows, I am not immune to such doubts.

But this same experience of *no separation* has stood at the heart of the world's mystical–spiritual traditions for thousands of years. Regardless of their cultural differences, their core message has been the same. Beyond our ordinary sense of being a separate self, with all its attendant anxieties, there is another state of consciousness, characterized by a profound inner knowing that we are inseparably one in a transcendent Whole.

In the Hindu, Jain, and Sikh traditions, this state is called *moksha,* meaning liberation from the illusion of our separateness. Buddhists speak of awakening to our true nature as *nirvana* or *satori.* In Sufism, *fanaa* means annihilation of the separate self. In Christianity, the same state is called *the kingdom of God, the kingdom of heaven,* and *eternal life.* Nor is this idea confined to mystical or spiritual traditions. This mode of transpersonal as distinct from ego-centred consciousness can arise in any context. Psychologists today often refer to it as *non-dual* or *unity consciousness.*

Why the tidal wave of grief that so overwhelmed me should have delivered this experience—this *knowing* that we are one in an ocean of love, and that nothing, including death, can ever separate us from that love—remains for me a mystery. And the unforgettable gift of a broken heart.

∼

What happened on that morning when my heart broke open cannot adequately be captured in words. Our most profound inner experiences are like that. They are beyond words. They don't fit the subject–object categories of our language. And if we try to make them fit, we distort or degrade the experience itself. The best we can do is reach for a metaphor and say, "The experience is *like* such and such."

I think that's why Jesus spoke in parables. He never says what the kingdom of heaven *is*. Only what it is *like*. It's *like* a grain of mustard seed, he says, which is the tiniest of all seeds, but which, when sown in your field, can grow to become the greatest of shrubs. Or *like* leaven, which, when hidden in a lump of dough, causes the entire lump to rise.°

My experience was like that. Beyond all words. To say that I was engulfed by a tsunami of love, or that love dwells at the heart of the universe, or that my heart has become an ocean: all of these are merely metaphors. Who can say what the reality is? Even to say that "my heart broke open" is a curious attempt to describe the indescribable. I could as easily say that "my heart was broken into." It was a *break-in*. The intensity of my grief jimmied open my heart, overwhelmed its defences, and allowed this ocean of love to break in upon me. The ocean of love that was engulfing Bella, to which she was returning or into which she was dissolving, was at the same time engulfing me. We were somehow together in this ocean of love.

The ocean metaphor had begun to emerge and take shape for me twenty years earlier. Bella and I were living by the sea—in a Greek-style house we had designed and built atop a 300-foot cliff overlooking the Pacific—near the village of Sumner on the outskirts of Christchurch. We called the house *Halcyon,* meaning *calm* or *peaceful.* It's the name of a bird that, in Greek legend, is said to calm the sea in order to incubate its eggs on a floating nest.

The design-and-build enterprise was for both of us immensely satisfying. I am something of a frustrated architect who, over the years, has drawn many house plans. Now I had the chance to do it for real, albeit with the help of qualified professionals. My intention was to have as many rooms as possible with dimensions that expressed the Golden Ratio—the ratio of 1 to 1.618 derived from the relationship between numbers in the Fibonacci series identified by ancient Greek mathematicians. For some reason no one understands, this ratio is found throughout nature—from the dimensions of DNA's double-helix molecule, to the distribution of seeds on a sunflower's head, to the spiral arms of distant galaxies. Our satisfaction culminated when, on the evening we moved into Halcyon, a brilliant rainbow appeared over the ocean directly in front of us. And when, a few days later, a good friend, Peter Masters, who at that time was one of Australasia's leading potters, came to see what we had built. Within minutes of setting foot in the house, and with no prompting from either Bella or me, he exclaimed, "My God, you've designed this according to the Golden Ratio."

The house was well named. Those years by the sea included our most halcyon days, shared always with one or another dog whom Bella may have loved even more than she loved me. Laugharne (pronounced "Larn") was an adorable mutt named after a seaside town in Wales that once was home to Dylan Thomas. Laugharne ended his days at Halcyon and was replaced by Ollie, an overweight Yellow Lab with a greater capacity for empathy than any human I have ever known. If today I am still reasonably fit for my years, it is due in no small measure to these beloved animals, who required that I take them for long walks along the clifftops twice each day.

During these walks by the sea I began to experience, on sporadic and unpredictable occasions, my first glimpses of this state of *unity consciousness*. Moments when the boundaries that define my usual sense of being a separate self seemed to dissolve into a Oneness that encompassed and included everything. Moments when I knew that I am inseparably one with something infinitely greater than myself.

Because these moments are timeless, it's hard to know how long such experiences lasted. I think they were fleeting. Always they were blissful. And always unexpected. Nothing I did, or could do, would induce them—though I suspect that my long-term practice of meditation may have loaded the dice in this direction.

To use a different metaphor, it was as if the software with which I am programmed to experience my world (written in the syntax of spoken language, which separates everything into *either–or*) was instantly replaced by a different program that sees everything as belonging to a unitary Whole. Or, in the language of Martin Buber, the Hasidic mystic and philosopher, the world of *It*, the world of separate things, suddenly became transparent to the *Thou* in which all things have their being.°

Such experiences may be unusual, but they are not uncommon. For millennia, people of diverse cultures have reported experiencing this life-changing shift in consciousness. Transpersonal psychologists today refer to these experiences by different names, such as peak experiences, transcendent events, and spontaneous spiritual awakenings. I call them *moments of connection*.

Because these moments are, for me, so extraordinary, where they occurred is indelibly inscribed in my memory. Which, as often as not, was while walking Laugharne or Ollie on the clifftops above the sea. On one such occasion, I was following a path across an open expanse of grassland. The morning sun was already well above the ocean horizon. Seagulls were playing in the updrafts. And the summer sky had that tingling clarity I have known only in New Zealand. Suddenly it all became transparent, exactly as Buber had described, to a *Thou*, a *Presence*, a *Unity* beyond all words, to which we all belong. And in that moment, I was filled with joy.

Another time, again by the sea, I was walking with Ollie on the Sumner Esplanade, near the beachside restaurants. It was winter. An early morning mist, almost a light rain, filled the air. No one else was around, although at one point the scent of freshly brewed coffee hung in the moist morning air. And then a solitary seagull flew low across the Esplanade, directly toward me. And for a fleeting moment, as it drew near, I saw God in the face of that seagull. *I swear I saw God in the face of a seagull.* And again I was filled with joy.

My experience in such moments can only be described as one of *Presence*. I am in every sense aware of my world. But the separate objects that normally constitute my world become transparent to a Presence that fills and unites them all. Like Moses' burning bush, the world is aflame with the same Presence that infuses everything. In the world of *It*, there is always separation. But when *It* becomes transparent to *Thou*, there is only Presence. And the place on which I stand is holy ground. Which is why this experience so often feels like a *religious* experience. The Presence in which everything participates feels like *divine* Presence.

Experiences like these formed the background out of which the ocean metaphor emerged—on another morning walk with Ollie. We had followed the clifftop track as far as we could, descended almost to sea level, and then climbed again up a long pathway to Nicholson Park. Near the top of that ascending path sits a bench, overlooking Sumner Bay, where I would often pause to catch my breath and take in the view. On this occasion, looking down at the bay, I watched sea swells turn into waves that crested and then broke as they neared the shore. Each wave was distinctly identifiable. I could follow its course. I could even, if I wished, give each a name. "Here comes Harry. And look, right behind, there's Susie." But however distinct and seemingly separate each wave appeared to be, it was of course just the ocean waving.

And that, it seemed to me, is what I am. And what each of us is. Whatever name we give to the *One*, to the *Unity*, to that unnameable *Mystery* to which in moments of connection we know that we belong, we are like waves on the ocean. The ocean is waving; *the Mystery is Merving.* As the ocean rises and falls in an infinity of waves, so the One is forever giving rise to this world of "ten thousand things."°

So on the morning Bella died, when I found myself engulfed by love, the experience was immediately shaped, and then expressed, by this metaphor. A tsunami, a tidal wave of love, swept over me. Bella and I together were dissolving, drowning, and at the same time borne up in an ocean of love. This is who we are. This is the fundamental nature of reality. This is the immensity of who we are. We are ripples, waves, manifestations in time and space, of an infinitely vast and timeless ocean of love that some call God.

If only I could more often remember who I really am. If only I could let go of, or at least see behind, all my ego-identities and remember who I am. Let go of all my constrictions. Let go into this ocean of love and let it flow through me. But I don't know how to *do* that. The "me" that thinks it is the *doer* keeps getting in the way. And then in moments of grace, in unexpected moments of connection, walking by the sea or kneeling in grief beside my beloved Bella, it is *done unto me.* Why or how I do not know. But in those moments, I and the ocean of love are one.

∾ SIX ∾

SHADES OF GREY

If only it were that simple. Just a matter of discovering, in some openhearted moment of connection, that there is no separation, not even in death, and that we are all inseparably one in an ocean of love. We are walking along, minding our business, when suddenly we see what we hadn't seen before. Like Archimedes, sitting in his ancient Greek bath, shouting "Eureka!" when Archimedes' Principle dawned on him.° Now we can never *not see* what we have seen to be true. It forever changes how we see our world. And perhaps how we live our life.

But it's *not* that simple. At least not for me. My mind will not leave well enough alone. It insists on trying to make rational sense of what I know intuitively to be true. And it's capable of wreaking havoc. Casting into doubt everything that, just a breath ago, seemed so self-evidently true.

"An ocean of love, you say. Love at the heart of the universe." The challenge begins. Like some courtroom prosecutor, my mind begins its cross-examination. "Excuse me, Merv. Have you forgotten Auschwitz and Hiroshima and Rwanda and Srebrenica and Aleppo and all the other hate-driven atrocities that have punctuated our human story for thousands of years? You can be forgiven a degree of poetic licence. But what you are proposing is nothing but a fairy tale. And as for there being *no separation*, even in death—well, I understand that, in the midst of grief, this may be a comforting idea. But it's clearly a non-rational statement, for which there is no empirical evidence whatsoever."

All of which and more I've been telling myself since Bella died. My initial turmoil of confusion and self-doubt has diminished, but what feels like an internal civil war between my heart and my head continues. It's a conflict between what I need to believe and what I can accept as credible. Between the competing truth-claims of two quite different sides of me—an intuitively perceptive heart and a rationally discursive mind—each trying in its own way to assimilate what I've been experiencing.

The battle lines for the conflict were drawn long ago. Raised in a liberal Protestant home, I had, as a youth, happily believed that Easter was true. But theological training quickly put an end to any literal interpretation of those Biblical accounts. So my mind moved on. Beguiled for a time by the "New Age" thinking of the 1970s. Later, fascinated by tales of reincarnation and near-death experiences. Most recently, immersed in the thinking of theoretical physicists and other scientists who suggest that consciousness may be more than just the chattering of neurons in our brain.° But my mind is also steeped in the more fashionable belief (fashionable at least in secular societies like New Zealand), affirmed by many with astonishing certainty, that nothing of our individuality could possibly survive death. So, on that Friday morning, overwhelmed by grief, my mind was fertile ground in which this intractable debate could take root and blossom into open conflict and an agony of inner turmoil.

Bella and I sometimes spoke of our impending demise and the virtually unthinkable prospect of saying our final goodbye. But we never discussed whether we might continue to be together in some way after death. Bella saw no point in speculating about matters that could not be settled one way or the other. How many angels could dance on the head of a pin was of no interest to her. And I was quietly envious of her wisdom. A wisdom both profound and practical, often noted by those who knew her well, that was more endearing than my more-academic learning.

Which isn't to say that Bella didn't have her own unusual sensitivities that sometimes delivered astonishing experiences. Like the ghost she encountered in the large three-storey house that we rented for a while on Oriole Gardens in Toronto. One night, immediately upon our getting into bed, Bella said quietly and with no evident alarm, "There's a man looking in the window." Which was impossible, since our bedroom was on the second floor. Unless he was fifteen feet tall. Besides which, I saw nothing at all. But Bella insisted, quietly describing him as dressed in rather formal late-19th-century attire, complete with top hat. He said nothing and did nothing other than stare at Bella. Then he vanished. If that had been the end of it, we might both have dismissed the apparition as nothing more than the play of shadows on the window. But this 19th-century gentleman returned in precisely the same way on several successive nights, with his arrival sometimes announced by the sound of a horse-drawn carriage clattering over a cobblestone street. Bella tried speaking softly to him, but received no reply. I suggested that she just quietly send him her love. There was still no response. Just his vacant stare. Although I neither saw nor heard anything, I had no doubt that Bella's experience was real. Yes, she was known sometimes to embellish her stories. But she would never have concocted anything as fanciful as this.

This particular story ended when Sheila, an extremely sensitive friend who knew of Bella's apparition, noticed a framed photograph hanging in a front room of our house. It was an old-fashioned, sepia-toned portrait of a family—mother, father, and six or eight children—standing in a formal, Victorian-era pose. We had found it a year or two earlier, amid a clutter of things in the basement of this rental house. Because it was beautifully framed in oak, we chose to hang it on a wall and didn't give it a second look. But this time, Sheila looked more closely at the picture and asked Bella if perhaps the father of this family was her ghost. Which, upon closer scrutiny, Bella declared to be the case. The Victorian gentleman in the photo was indeed the man appearing in our bedroom window. And from that moment, from the moment he was *recognized*, he was never seen again.

Despite my desire to make sense of everything, I was not prepared to speculate about this story. I might sometimes resurrect it as entertaining table talk at dinner parties, but its implications were too bizarre to consider seriously. Not so, however, when it comes now to wondering what to make of my surprising and recurring sense of Bella's after-death presence. Or of the messages emerging, as if from her, in my early morning practice of deep listening. The tension that has always existed between my head and my heart erupts easily into open conflict, leaving me with two options. I can accept what my heart intuits to be true and risk being thought an irrational fool. Or I can dismiss all such intuitions as a cruel anomaly that will one day be fully understood in scientific terms.

In the hours and days immediately following Bella's death, it was no contest. My emotional need trumped all rationality. I needed to stake my life less on what my mind thought was plausible and more on the intuitions flooding my now-open heart. And be willing to embrace, without embarrassment, whatever contradiction existed between the two. Initially, whether or not anything of us survives death scarcely entered my mind. All such intellectual considerations vanished in the face of what seemed so incontrovertibly true. That death is not the end. That Bella lives on in an eternal realm. And that we will one day be together again.

But in today's world—in a secular society lacking transcendence or depth—that conviction, that hope, is difficult to maintain. Soon enough, my rational mind re-emerged to torment me with its doubts. The fear that my experience of Bella's presence might be nothing more than wishful thinking. An understandable delusion created by my mind to ease the pain of facing the reality that she was finally and forever gone. And always, lurking in the background, the now-familiar anger that comes and goes and comes again. Like a dull complaint that rarely surfaces in words, but harbours one soul-destroying thought. If this is how it ends—if all that we have been and become is finally reduced to nothing more than ashes and to memories that will fade and disappear—then perhaps the Preacher, in the Book of Ecclesiastes, had it right when he lamented long ago that, unlike the living and the dead, "most fortunate of all are those who are not yet born."[o]

Despite the blissful insights and comforting assurances with which I have been blessed, the truth is that many of my days since Bella died, especially during the early weeks and months, have been coloured by this mental torment in seemingly endless shades of grey. Reflected in journal entries like the following:

> Yesterday was an emotionally chaotic day. When, in the morning, I sat to be with Bella, I was filled with terrible doubts. The loss of Bella feels like an amputation, as if something that was very much a part of me has been cut away. What if this sense of her presence is nothing but a

kind of *phantom-limb* illusion—a temporary anomaly as my mind redraws the map of its new reality?

Then, when I went to bed last night, I was again uplifted by a joyous sense of Bella's presence, complete with laughter. It felt so good, and I was hugely grateful for being given this experience.

Now, since awakening this morning, I've been trying to shape some credible understanding of my experience. What if the life of each of us is like that of a single pine needle in the vast foliage of a giant pine tree? Each needle is alive and makes its contribution to the life of the tree. But the life of the needle is not its own. It's an expression of the tree's life. And when that needle dies, the life of the tree continues. Could we say that each needle's contribution to the tree lives on after that needle dies? By analogy, then, what if we are each a local expression of a universal field of consciousness? And what if, as some scientists are suggesting, *information* belongs to the essential nature of reality?° Could it be that the unique "package of information" that was Bella lives on as an imprint on this field of consciousness? Such that her presence can still be felt by those with whom an inner connection has been made?

Such questions, I suspect, can never be answered in rational or scientific terms. But I feel a certain urgency in wanting to find plausible support for believing that Bella's continuing presence is real and not a phantom-limb illusion.

This morning, as I sat and listened in my customary manner, the following message took shape in my mind:

*Our continuing presence beyond death is inconceivable
    to your mind.
It is impossible to imagine in any credible way.*

*But such things can be known in experience—beyond
   the mind.
So go there now, and I will be with you,
closer than your breathing.
When your own breathing stops in death, then you will
   truly know.
Until then, hold to the conviction
that what you have sometimes glimpsed to be true is
   actually so.*

Then, in this morning's e-mail, was an article sent
by a friend. It referenced a number of eminent scientists
who have pointed to the possibility that consciousness
may indeed survive death. One is Robert Lanza, an adjunct
professor at Wake Forest University School of Medicine,
who for many years has been at the frontier of stem cell
research. In a 2007 article and subsequent 2009 book, he
proposed the idea of a "biocentric universe" according to
which consciousness creates the universe, not the other way
around. Space and time are only mental constructs or "tools
of our mind."° And because consciousness exists outside
the constraints of space and time, death construed as the
extinction of consciousness does not exist.

Another was German physicist Hans-Peter Dürr
(1929–2014), for many years the Executive Director of
the Max Planck Institute for Physics and Astrophysics in
Munich, who suggested that a body–soul duality may be
an extension of the wave–particle duality of subatomic
particles. Perhaps, he suggested, as a particle *writes* its
information on its wave function, so our brain may be like
a floppy disk on which data is saved and then uploaded
into a spiritual quantum field. When we die, the physical
disk is destroyed, but the data of consciousness lives on.
"[T]his world," said Dürr, "is actually just the material level
that is comprehensible. The beyond is an infinite reality

that is much bigger. ... Our lives ... are encompassed, surrounded, by the afterworld already. The body dies but the spiritual quantum field continues. In this way, I am immortal."°

I find none of this persuasive. I can't imagine any possible scientific validation for the belief that consciousness survives death. But I'm encouraged by scientists who do not simply dismiss out of hand any possibility that consciousness may survive the death of our physical brain.

The moods of my grief change like the weather. Today is not a typical spring day. It is cold and grey. Threatening rain. And my mood matches that. My grief (if I can even call it that) this morning is dry and cynical. Bella seems far away; perhaps (I am afraid to say it) even *gone.* There are no tears, and my heart feels closed. The day that stretches ahead looks bleak and empty. There are things I have to do and people I have to meet. But the day looks bleak and empty nonetheless.

Faith is a dangerous and misunderstood word in today's world. *Trust* may be a better word. But by whatever name, it's what I want and need. I want so very much to know and trust that Bella is a living aspect of that Intimate Presence of which I am sometimes aware. To believe that all that she was and is continues as a kind of imprint on the fabric of eternity. That she is incorporated (as we all are, if only we knew it) into that Beloved Mystery that some of us still call God. And that our love, our connection, continues as an unbroken thread that is part of the fabric of eternity. One of the countless fibres that make up the enormous heart of God.

But this morning, my educated, rational, skeptical mind, and my oh-so-tender heart, were as cold and grey as the weather itself. Given my cynicism, I had to push myself to sit and seek some kind of contact with Bella. And while, just a few minutes earlier, I would have said that "there are no tears and my heart feels closed," now, the instant I sat down, I broke into sobbing, saying aloud "I am so afraid of losing you, my love. I don't ever want to lose you." And then these words took shape in my mind:

My poor sweet darling;
you are in such distress.
But you need never lose me, my love.
I am so very, very close to you, even now.
I wish you could know—not just believe, but know—how it
*   really is.*
I am in fact closer to you now than ever was possible in our
*   earthly life together.*
Please know that all is well.
I am always with you, and there is nothing to fear.

———————————

My days continue to feel empty, grey and colourless. I wonder if this is how it will be for the rest of my life. Last night, my fantasy was of becoming a monk. Living a simple life in a monastery and spending each day in prayer and meditation. It seemed a way to retreat from the world of everything that I had shared with Bella and am now having so much difficulty facing without her. Then, as I sat and inwardly listened, this is what emerged:

Your mind is such a troublemaker;
it keeps muddying the water.
It takes what is really quite clear
and turns it into confusion.
Trust your heart's perception.
It sees directly.

Its knowing is not muddied by any desire to be intellectually
    credible.
It is simply present to what is.
Stick to your practice;
suspend your frenetic thinking,
and open your heart.

Enough! No more words! Simply be with me now.

As the days tick by, the waves of grief sweep through me less often and with less intensity—as if, of necessity, I am discovering that I can live without Bella. The house is hugely empty, and there are times when I miss her intensely. But life goes on. All of which concerns me greatly. I don't *want* to get along without her; I don't *want* her to be reduced to a mere memory; I don't *want* my broken heart to heal—for fear that I will really lose her and she will finally be gone as a living presence in my life. This was the background to what I received this morning.

Good morning, darling.
I am still here—always with you.
Your mind plays tricks on you—tortures you with doubt—
which is its purpose—to constantly assess your situation in life
    as realistically as possible.
But, as you know, there is a kind of truth that is beyond the
    mind,
beyond words, beyond rationality—
a knowing that belongs not to the mind but to the heart.
All you can do, my love, is listen to your heart;
that is where you will find me.

As I reflected on this, it seemed so clear that the mind and heart—like science and religion, the rational and the spiritual, empirical knowledge and intuitive insight—are but complementary modes of knowing. Both must be employed in a continuing state of tension. To try to remove that tension by discarding one or the other is to be less than human.

Memories are in my mind; Bella lives in my heart. I can't explain that, but I can experience it. She has taken up residence in my heart. And now a new way of being together is possible.

The past twenty-four hours have been very emotional. Last evening, I watched the television reports of the 13 November terrorist attacks that killed 130 people in Paris. And this morning, because of time pressure to prepare for our Sunday Gathering,° I didn't "sit" to be with Bella as my custom has been. But early this evening, prompted by a sense of her presence, I did so.

I am here, my love.
It has been a tiring and emotional day for you.
But you can rest a while now—here with me.
You are all surrounded by so much love and compassion.
Life in the world is a hard school,
and we learn what we learn.
But always you are held in love,
with compassion for all that you must suffer.
I love you, Meru.

After receiving this, I thought: there are two options. Either this really is a transmission from Bella, or it's a creation of my own imagining. If the latter, then it represents how I *want* my reality to be, what I *want* to believe. And, if that's the case, since no empirical evidence or rational argument can possibly settle the issue, I might

just as well trust my own experience. I mean, faced with
these equally unverifiable but not implausible options,
why should I reject the one that offers hope and joy and
meaning, and choose instead a mindset that leaves me only
with Albert Camus' sense of "the Absurd"° or Jean-Paul
Sartre's "nausea"?°

    This evening, at least, that choice seems a no-brainer.

～

It seems clear to me that there are two ways of knowing, which yield two very
distinct kinds of truth. One comes from the workings of the rational mind.
The other, described in the message quoted earlier, has a different source:

> [T]here is a kind of truth that is beyond the mind,
> beyond words, beyond rationality—
> a knowing that belongs not to the mind but to the heart.

    This distinction has a long and reputable history. In the ancient languages
of India—the Sanskrit and Pali in which the sacred texts of Hinduism and
Buddhism were written—the distinction is fundamental. The Buddhist
concept of *prajna* refers to an immediate, spontaneous, hard-to-put-into-
words knowledge born of direct personal experience—sometimes translated
in Buddhist texts as "the greater knowing." *Vijnana,* on the other hand, refers
to the deliberate, intellectual analysis of reality. Although essential for dealing
with the world, it is, according to a traditional Buddhist saying, "the raft to be
abandoned upon reaching the other shore."°
    The same distinction was embedded in the language and culture of
Classical Greece, which informed Western civilization for more than two
thousand years. There is a kind of knowledge that is essential to navigate this
world successfully: a knowledge about what causes what in the natural order
of things. It requires a certain detachment from the world—approaching it
empirically and seeking verifiable explanations wherever possible. But this
by itself is not enough. To live a good and meaningful life, we also need
wisdom—which derives from a direct *inner* knowing of our place in the larger

scheme of things and yields what Martin Buber called "the inexpressible confirmation of meaning."°

In short, human cognition has long been seen as comprising two subsystems. One, objective–analytical–rational–empirical. The other, subjective–holistic–intuitive–experiential. To be fully and authentically human is to develop both. And hold them in creative balance.

With the advent of science in the 17th century, however, and continuing through the Age of Reason and assorted technology revolutions to the present day, this age-old appreciation of our two modes of knowing has been eroded to the point that, for many today, only the former has legitimacy. The *"knowing that belongs not to the mind but to the heart"* is discounted, if not dismissed entirely. Beguiled by our scientific discoveries, many of us are skeptical of any reality other than empirical data—that is, whatever can be observed, measured, and verified. The result: a culture in which not only God, but spiritual discernment and the sense of intrinsic meaning it delivers, have been declared dead.

And I am a product of that culture. At war with myself. Trying to do the impossible. To incorporate into a rational, evidence-based worldview what I have experienced as the gift of a broken heart.

I want so very much simply to trust this *"truth that is beyond the mind."* But my mind …

> *… is such a troublemaker;*
> *it keeps muddying the water.*
> *It takes what is really quite clear*
> *and turns it into confusion.*

I want so very much to have even a fraction of the faith of St. Thomas Aquinas (1225–1274 CE). A man of towering intellect who believed that God had created a divinely rational universe, he authored three enormous volumes—the *Summa Theologica*—that underpin Catholic theology to this day. His less-than-modest intention was to summarize the history of the cosmos and the meaning of life itself. But in his midforties, while still working on the third volume, he began to experience states of ecstasy. What today we would call *transcendent events*. And then, in December 1273, in the Chapel of Saint Nicholas in the Dominican convent of Naples, he had so powerful an experience of mystical knowing, such a profound opening of his heart into the Divine, that, from that moment, he set his pen aside and wrote no more. Although urged by associates to complete the *Summa,* Thomas insisted that he could not continue working on it, lamenting that "all that I have written [now] seems like straw to me."°

Far be it from me to liken my *inner knowing* to whatever it was that Thomas experienced. But I think I understand. And I would be content if I could only "*trust [my] heart's perception.*"

∼ SEVEN ∼
"WHAT IS THIS THING CALLED LOVE?"

One of my favourite jazz classics is Cole Porter's "What Is This Thing Called Love?"° It poses a perennial question for which there seems no simple answer. Yet here I am writing about it. Suggesting that we are all beings in love. Waves on an ocean of love. Speaking metaphorically, of course. But as if I know what I'm talking about.

The question came to the fore one night when I awoke from a dream and found myself *suffused with love*. I don't know how else to describe it. Not as overwhelming as the tidal wave that engulfed me on the morning Bella died, but similar. Something in me had *opened*. My boundaries had softened, giving way to a warm and radiant love that welled up within me.

The dream itself was as inexplicable as any other—though there was a time when, with a freshly minted graduate degree in psychology, I could have told you with youthful certainty exactly what it meant. Even now, I'm tempted to attribute meaning to the dream derived from all I've been experiencing since Bella died.

In the dream, Bella and I had just moved into a large stucco-clad house, on a street called Chapel Hill Road, in an unfamiliar section of a large city. As I was returning from some errand, I became disoriented and couldn't find my way home. Since I had promised Bella (who now, in the dream, had become a young girl) that I would take her to a new school she was to attend, I was increasingly concerned that I would be late. By the time I found the house, Bella had already left for school by herself. Feeling sorry for having failed to go with her, I set off for the school to see that she was all right.

That's when I woke up, feeling this big, warm, tender love. It was my love for Bella. But it was more than that. It was not just *my* love. It was a so-much-bigger love in which I was participating. As if it had taken me over and was being expressed *through* me. It's hard to find the words for this. Like trying to describe a colour. What's it like to experience yellow? What's it like to experience love? What exactly *is* this thing called love?

Then, as I generally do when I find myself awake in the early hours of the morning, I got up, put on my dressing gown, and went into the living room to meditate. Sitting there in the dark, I was still feeling this suffusion of love when I heard raindrops hitting the metal chimney of the fireplace. A heavy rainfall had begun. *And the sound of the raindrops opened my heart still more.* I know that makes no sense. I can't explain it. But the downpour of rain felt like a downpour of love. It was not *my* love. It was not something I was *doing*. *It was being done to me.* As if love had found me—had through the dream found a point of entry, opened my heart, and was now flooding me. What had begun as a warm and tender love for Bella had burgeoned into this vast, all-embracing, and oh-so-gracious gift of love. What *is* this love? Where does it come from? How does it find us? As if it wants to make its home in us.

There was nothing I did, or could do, to make this happen. It was a gift. But I had the freedom, so it seemed, to say yes or no to it. To remain inwardly open and receptive, or to close down, toughen up, and reclaim my usual back-in-the-world sense of separateness. Though unaware of doing so, I must have chosen the former—for, when I returned to bed an hour later, I was still held in the blissful embrace of this love.

∽

When, years ago, I and a small group of friends were immersed for a while in the teachings of G.I. Gurdjieff, it was commonplace to say that "life is a conspiracy to put us to sleep." To render us less conscious, less present than we might be. Whether Gurdjieff actually said that, I don't know. But I think it's true. It's all too easy to go through life on automatic, in a kind of dumbed-down state of consciousness. But now, in the light of my unexpected grief experiences, I suspect that life may also sometimes conspire to wake us up. In particular, to awaken us to love. It invites us, nudges us, prompts us. And sometimes breaks open our heart and floods us with *whatever this is that we call love. Whether via a dream, or carried on raindrops, or in tears of grief when suddenly one morning we find ourselves in the presence of death.*

Again, these are only words that explain nothing. What can one say? It's as if on such occasions I slip into another mode of consciousness. One in which my ordinary sense of separateness dissolves. Time becomes so condensed as to scarcely exist beyond the present moment. And in this present moment I am not *doing* anything. Not thinking. Not planning. There is no mental chatter. Just a vast inner silence and spaciousness filled with nothing but the sound of raindrops or the unspeakable anguish of grief, accompanied by a love that fills the universe.

There may be nothing unusual in this. Our everyday separative consciousness may simply be so well established as our default position that we are surprised when something in the region of our heart opens and we find ourselves in this different mode of consciousness. William James, the 19th-century father of modern psychology, famously said as much in his book *The Varieties of Religious Experience.*

> [O]ur normal waking consciousness ... is but one special type of consciousness, whilst all about it, parted from it by the filmiest of screens, there lie potential forms of consciousness entirely different.°

When, for reasons I never understand, this "filmiest of screens" dissolves and I am granted entrée to this other domain, it comes as both gift and blessing. It comes to lead me out, however fleetingly, from all this anxious preoccupation with my separate self. It comes to remind me that I am inseparably one with a reality infinitely greater than myself. And always it fills me with a joy and a love unknown to me in my ordinary state.

These "peak experiences" or "transcendent events" may occur more frequently in our later years. Certainly that accords with my experience. But it seems to me life is never devoid, even in our younger years, of invitations to this deeper love. It's as if we are hard-wired to respond to certain built-in *attractors* that we can't avoid. As if the game is rigged. Life is replete with ordinary experiences in which is hidden a potential opening to this other domain of consciousness. We might think of these as life's *little loves* that invite us to close the gap that separates us. Our friendships, our sexual attractions, our family loves, our partnerships, our attraction to beauty, our love of nature, and so on. Little loves whose attractive power makes itself felt in countless ways to remind us that we belong to someone or something beyond ourselves. Then, with the power to open our hearts, they conspire to alter our life trajectory and, in due course, return us to the One from which, or from whom, it is impossible ever finally to be separate.

The ancient Greeks were wise enough to assign different names to these attractors. *Eros* referred to romantic sexual love, though Plato used it to refer as well to our love of beauty. *Storge* (pronounced "STOR-gay") is the love of parents for their children. *Philia* is the love between friends and comrades-in-arms. And *pragma* is the practical partnership variety of love that often exists between long-married couples. These are part of the ordinary fabric of our lives. Part of being human. It's hard to imagine anyone not feeling, at some point in their life, the attractive pull of at least one of them. But they are always conditional. In order for such love to thrive, those we love must meet our expectations. And if they fail to deliver a measure of reciprocity, these types of love can quickly wane.

But hidden in them all is the possibility of our opening to a deeper love that is universal and unconditional. A love that feels as if it has been there all along, at a deeper level of ourselves. Beyond all expectations, it just *is*. We cannot choose it, cultivate it, or in any sense make it happen. It comes to us unbidden, in the sound of raindrops or in tears of grief. It opens our heart, and delivers us, however briefly, into this other domain of consciousness. The Greeks called it *agape* (pronounced "a-GAH-pay"). That's the word used when the Bible says that "God is love."° It feels to me like an ocean of love. Perhaps we could simply call it *Big Love*, or *Love-with-a-capital-L*.

∾

Since childhood, I've had a love affair with trees. They have consistently been for me a strong attractor. One of my little loves. At my family's summer cottage on the shores of Georgian Bay, I liked nothing more than to walk, often with my mother, through the surrounding woods. Or lie in the hammock hung beneath a large White Pine tree, gazing up at the blue summer sky through the soft wispy green of the pine's foliage.

It was this attraction, this love for trees, that led me to study forestry in my first year of university. Until that summer (I was only in my late teens) when, while working as a forest ranger in the wilderness of northern Canada, I would often sit, at the end of the day, by the water's edge and watch the sun go down, silhouetting the forest on the far side of the lake. Those moments were filled with a profound stillness and an awesome power. The haunting call of a loon or the unexpected thwack of a beaver's tail might pierce the silence, but the stillness remained unbroken. I would watch as the crimson sky darkened, filling with a million stars. The rising moon would work its magic. Multicoloured northern lights, pink and green and white, would splash and crackle across the sky. And always, in the distance, the howling of the wolves.

I found it inconceivable that all this was just a cosmic accident. The entire universe seemed pregnant with meaning. I could *feel* it all around me. I could almost reach out and *touch* the meaning. I couldn't get my mind around it. I couldn't put words to it. But I would have bet my life that there was far more there than met the eye. And it changed my life.

My love affair with trees, with its hidden portal to something Beyond, has continued to this day. On a recent visit to Toronto, I travelled north to Algonquin Park to feast again on the beauty of Ontario's northern lakes and woodlands. It was mid-October. Maples and poplars, aspens and oaks, resplendent in their autumnal hues, were interspersed throughout the pine forests. Early one morning, walking near the campground through a light dusting of early snow, I was suddenly and inwardly moved by one of these trees. It was a very ordinary tree. Nothing special. But as I walked beside it, we connected. How else can I describe it? Something in me opened. Tears welled up in me. And we found ourselves—the tree and I—*together in Love.*

I suspect that's not unusual. How can anyone be so hard-hearted as to be immune to nature's touch? As to never feel their deep kinship with nature? Their belonging to this larger Whole? Can anyone be so inwardly disconnected that nature never opens them, a little or a lot, to whatever this is that we call love?

There is a book of poetry, still in my library after forty-five years, titled

Anerca. It's an English translation of Inuit poetry. For the indigenous people of the Arctic, the word *anerca* has three meanings. As a noun, it means *spirit.* As a verb, it means *to breathe* and *to write poetry.* Breathing and writing poetry are synonymous. Both are expressions of the human spirit. One of these poems speaks powerfully to me of my experience:

> Great Sea
> Sends me drifting,
> Moves me,
> Weed in a river am I.
> Great Nature
> Sends me drifting,
> Moves me,
> Moves my inward parts with joy.
>
> The great sea
> Has sent me adrift
> It moves me as the weed in a great river,
> Earth and the great weather
> Move me,
> Have carried me away
> And move my inward parts with joy.°

Some of these loves emerge so naturally, it seems we are hard-wired to experience them. Most parents, for instance, bond with their newborn children and feel a powerfully protective love for them. What the Greeks called *storge.* We are a species whose children, in order to survive, need parental love and care for many years. And we are programmed to provide it. But sometimes—just sometimes—this everyday little love, so much a part of being a parent that we easily take it for granted, opens our heart, melts our boundaries, and becomes a Love so big, so immense, that it is hard to bear.

One such occasion is forever imprinted on my memory: the day I sat at the hospital beside my eldest son, Mark, when he was only four years old.

He had undergone minor surgery and, having just emerged from the anaesthetic, was sick and in pain. Tears came to my eyes. He was so small, so young. I would gladly have taken all his pain and carried it for him. And I could not. What was given him to suffer was his alone. Each in the privacy of our own experience, something passed between us. He probably has no memory of that moment, but for me it was unforgettable—the now-familiar sensation of my heart opening into a far deeper Love that seemed to envelop us both. Into this Big Love that the Greeks called *agape*.

Another such occasion also comes to mind. Carol and I and our three young sons were at the family cottage on Georgian Bay. It was evening, and the children were in bed. Looking forward to this quiet time, I had lit a fire in the stone fireplace and settled comfortably into the big wicker armchair when I heard our second son, Bruce, quietly sobbing. He was seven years old. Through his tears he confessed that, earlier that afternoon, he had, with a pellet gun, shot and killed a sparrow perched in a tree. Overcome with guilt and sorrow, he could not now erase from his mind the image of the tiny bird he had killed. How my heart went out to him! Gathering him into my arms, I carried him to the big wicker chair and held him as we quietly cried together. BIG LOVE! Very, very BIG LOVE! My heart had been torn open. And far beyond my everyday protective love for him, and whatever his seven-year-old love was for me, we were for those few minutes wrapped together in that Love-with-a-capital-L which knows no bounds.

And then there is romantic love. Driven by that unrelenting sexual attraction which can wreak such havoc and cause such pain—and at the same time open us to depths of intimacy that perhaps can be reached in no other way. Like the protective impulse we feel toward our children, this attractor is hard-wired into us. First introduced 500 million years ago when evolution chanced upon this novel means of reproduction, it proved so successful as to issue in the Cambrian Explosion of life-forms that have populated the world ever since.

But it's more than just a biological necessity. It's an attractor first felt as "puppy love" when we are still prepubescent children. And then maturing into what can sometimes be the vehicle for a connection of such intensity as to usher us into realms of transcendent experience that forever change our lives.

The puppy-love stage began for me at the still-tender age of nine. Anne McIntyre lived just up the street from where I lived on Kingsgarden Road in a Toronto suburb known as The Kingsway. Even at that young age, my attraction to her felt "naughty." When our classmates corralled us one afternoon and forced us to kiss, I prayed every night for weeks thereafter that my parents would not find out. Then, with the fickleness that often characterizes romantic love, my attentions turned to Joan Dalrymple. She lived farther from my home, which meant that after school and on Saturdays I had to "go exploring." Riding my bike to the far side of The Kingsway, I would repeatedly, and as nonchalantly as possible, pass her home on Brentwood Road, hoping we might meet.

By the time I was twelve and the first surges of testosterone were making themselves felt, the power of this attractor began heating up. Though she didn't know it at the time, Sharon Moore was another of my secret loves. And she was gorgeous. She lived on Strath Avenue, close enough to where I lived that I could easily stroll past her house, ever hopeful that I might see her. Then, one Saturday evening, my wildest dream came true. I was invited to a house party at the home of Charlie Wells, just two doors up the street from where I lived. And there was Sharon. At some point in the evening, I mustered the courage to ask her to dance. She said yes. And we danced—cheek to cheek! It was only one dance: I couldn't handle any more. In a kind of swoon, I excused myself and left the party, wanting nothing more than to savour for as long as possible the lingering feel of Sharon's cheek against mine.

Despite the hormonal turbulence of teenage years, and even after four years of steady dating, Carol and I were still virgins when we married at twenty-one. Sexual intimacy beyond a certain point was a taboo drummed into me ever since my brother Ron, five years older than I was, brought shame to our family with a shotgun wedding. Little did I know at the time that my parents *and* my maternal grandparents had entered the not-so-holy estate of matrimony in the same way. But however far back that family tradition might have extended, it ended with me.

Were Carol and I in love? I think so. Though now, in retrospect, it seems that we were little more than children, unprepared for all that marriage entails. On the inside of her wedding ring were inscribed the words "Love never fails." But it did. Postpartum depression and my own self-centred preoccupation with my studies and career took their toll. Not to mention the so-called sexual revolution of the 1960s. We parted company in 1969, after thirteen years of marriage and my three-year on-and-off affair with Bella. Strangely, as my capacity for love has matured over the years since then, my love for Carol now, despite our having only occasional contact, feels not only different but deeper than it was nearly fifty years ago.

With that maturation too has emerged the astonishing capacity of sexual love to open me more and more to what I am here calling Love-with-a-capital-L. Like other attractors or little loves, it too can sometimes be a doorway to the transcendent and transpersonal. Early in my relationship with Bella, there were occasions, beautiful and scary moments when, in making love, I would quite lose myself. All boundaries would dissolve, no sense of "me" remaining—melting, flowing, drifting weightless in the depths of some engulfing ocean—only to awaken with a start, like a drowning man who knows he's going down and makes one last attempt to hold to something solid. So I would make for shore, reaching for the boundaries of that dry familiar land I know is me.

Jenny Wade, a former faculty member at the Institute of Transpersonal Psychology in Palo Alto who is currently with the California Institute of Integral Studies, has studied this phenomenon, and in 2004 published findings based on the accounts of ninety-one individuals who, in the course of sexual relations, found themselves in an altered state of consciousness akin to what would be recognized as a classical mystical experience.° Other researchers have reported similar accounts. In one of these, a man is quoted as saying, "when we make love, it's like I disappear."° And in another, a woman says, "There is a unitive energy where the two truly become one. And once in a while you transcend even that, and you become one with the universe. … [It's a] doorway you pass through into something beyond, something transcendent."°

That too has been my experience—though only rarely do I risk love's depths. As if in letting go, surrendering my boundaries, abandoning myself and all my efforts to maintain control, I might lose myself in some much larger and inclusive union and never find myself again.

~

Long before Western societies made the dubious move to base marriage on the uncertain vicissitudes of romantic love, it had for centuries been arranged to serve purely pragmatic ends. Marriage was a working partnership that, over years of being together, working together, and raising children together, might, as a kind of bonus, issue in a kind of love that the Greeks called *pragma*. It is wonderfully exemplified in stories Bella loved to tell about her maternal grandparents.

Samuel and Esther met for the first time on their wedding day, under the *chuppah*, in a synagogue in Minsk, Ukraine. Samuel was twenty-seven. Esther was twenty-two. The marriage had been arranged between the respective families by a matchmaker. The year was 1903—the first of four horrific years during which anti-Semitic pogroms swept northern Ukraine. Jews were given an ultimatum: convert to Christianity or be expelled from Russia. Some took up arms to protect their families and property, but they were no match for their persecutors. In a 1905 pogrom, 54 Jews were killed in Minsk and as many as 2500 in Odessa. On the day following Easter, priests in Kishinev led a mob in massacring Jews, while the cry "Kill the Jews" was taken up all over the city.

Amid this mayhem, Bella's mother, Annie, was born in 1904, and her uncle Norman in 1905. While they were still little more than newborns, their father, Samuel, fled the pogroms and escaped to London, promising to arrange for Esther to follow when he was settled. Months went by, but, apart from learning of his London address, Esther heard nothing more from him. So, girding her loins, in 1906, with her two infant children, two brass Sabbath candlesticks, and little more than the clothes on their backs, Esther set off for London in hopes of finding Sam. Just how a woman in such circumstances, speaking nothing but Yiddish and perhaps a smattering of Russian, found her way from Minsk to London is utterly beyond me. But in due course, she was knocking on the door at the London address she'd been given. And when Samuel appeared at the door, she is said to have asked somewhat querulously, "So, Samuel, do you remember me?"

From there to Wales, through two World Wars and an intervening Great Depression, Sam and Esther raised their family and welcomed their grandchildren in an atmosphere of *pragma*. Were they happy? That wasn't considered essential. It was enough that they had a working partnership. Sam was an orthodox and observant Jew, whom Bella regarded as a *rabbi* and from whom she learned all she needed to know about being Jewish. He spent most of his time in prayer, audibly intoning the prescribed prayers three times each day while davening and wearing the required *tefillin* or phylacteries. The latter—a set of small leather boxes containing parchment scrolls inscribed with verses from the Torah and tied to the head and arm with black leather straps—were an embarrassment to Bella whenever her gentile friends would see her grandfather so attired. Rather than explain the real reason for his appearance, she would say instead that he was a telephone line repairman and this strange garb was his equipment.

Only slightly less embarrassing to Bella was her zayde's (*zayde*, pronounced "zay-duh," is Yiddish for grandfather) refusal to speak English. That predilection served him well, allowing him to openly express the anti-gentile sentiments indelibly inscribed in him since the days of the pogroms. When his gentile neighbours would cheerily greet him, "Good morning, Mr. Sager," Sam would smilingly reply, "*Gai kaken oifen yam*"—which only other Jews would know meant "Go shit in the sea."

Esther too was someone to be reckoned with. Once, having prepared a bowl of *lokshen* or noodles for the evening meal, she declared that dinner was served and asked the family to gather at the table. Sam, however, was unresponsive. He was still davening and lost in prayer. So Esther took his serving of noodles and dumped them over his head. Without missing a beat, Bella said, he merely parted the noodles and continued davening and intoning his prayers.

Such is the love known as *pragma*. Other little loves must surely have been part of their experience as well. Certainly *storge*—a love for their children and grandchildren. And, hopefully, at least a touch of *eros*. But it was their working partnership, their *pragma*, that served them well for more than forty years. Whether any of these little loves ever served for them as portals into the Big Love that the Greeks called *agape* remains unknown. Such inner, spiritual matters are usually too private to be shared. Except in memoirs like this.

Esther died in 1947, aged sixty-six; Sam, in 1960, aged eighty-four. I knew them only through the stories Bella liked to tell. But I am grateful to them both for their astonishing faith and courage, without which Bella might never have been born. And for the profound influence they had in shaping the woman she became.

∼ EIGHT ∼
"ON THAT BUMPY ROAD TO LOVE"

For anyone who grows up in Wales, it's hard not to sing. And Bella loved to sing. Whether or not she had the voice for it was another matter.

One of her favourite stories was of singing in the school choir at Cyfarthfa Castle Grammar School. The school occupied an early 19th-century castle, complete with turrets and secret passageways, on the outskirts of Merthyr Tydfil. During one rehearsal, the choir director said, "I hear a drone," and proceeded to identify Bella as that drone. But she looked so happy and vivacious when she sang, she was permitted to continue occupying a place in the choir's front row, instructed now to only lip-synch the words without uttering a sound.

So Bella and I often sang together. Usually in the car. Always when heading off on a motor trip. Not five minutes out of town, we would launch into song. It was an expression of the freedom we felt in going on vacation. Now, as I prepare to narrate more of our love story, another song comes to mind: a Gershwin number that Bella insisted she would play at my funeral if I made my exit before her. Here is a portion of it.

> We may never, never meet again on that bumpy
>   road to love.
> Still I'll always, always keep the memory of
> The way you hold your knife,
> The way we danced till three,
> The way you changed my life—
> No, no, they can't take that away from me.°

The song is beautifully and painfully appropriate. Bella knew how bumpy our road to love had been. Full of exquisite joy, yes! And dreadful hurt. It couldn't have been otherwise, given who we were. Each crazy in our own way. Maybe there are couples for whom it's all smooth sailing. Who fall in love and spend a lifetime together without ever inflicting pain on each other. But that isn't how it was for us. Still, despite what we suffered, I will always, always, as the song declares, cherish the memories of the way we were. Of how she changed my life. They can't take that away from me.

~

When, on that snow-filled Valentine's Day in Toronto, we began our heart-thumpingly enticing journey down that bumpy road, it was another advance on what I see now as my life's trajectory. An opening to love fraught with often-chaotic conflict.

For the first three years of our relationship, it was an on-again, off-again affair. In a futile effort to maintain our marriages and not inflict broken homes on our children, we repeatedly called it off. Usually at my initiative. Only to give in again and again to an irresistible attraction.

We knew how seductive and illusory an affair can be. All candlelight and roses. And of course exciting. So lest we be making a huge mistake, we agreed to put ourselves in a situation where we would see each other as we truly were. Warts and all. We signed up for a weeklong workshop at Esalen—at that time the California mecca of humanistic psychology and home to some of its most illustrious therapists. We chose a workshop called "Our Masks and Ourselves" led by Claudio Naranjo.°

Esalen itself was hugely romantic. Situated on high cliffs along the Big Sur coast just south of Monterey, its rustic log buildings opened onto a wide expanse of lawn overlooking the Pacific. On that lawn, when we first arrived on a Sunday afternoon, an open-air concert was under way, featuring the fabled Indian sitar virtuoso Ravi Shankar, accompanied by the no-less-fabled tabla player Ali Akbar Khan. As the sound of classical Indian ragas and the scent of marijuana filled the summer air, Bella and I made love in a private nest atop the cliffs. Only to discover later that she had been lying bare-assed in a plot of poison ivy.

On that same evening, after dinner, as we were still finding our way around, we chanced upon another astonishing scene. Seated on cushions at the dining room's far end, robed in his customary attire, and speaking to a large assembled audience was none other than the Beatles' guru—Maharishi Mahesh Yogi.° This was beyond our wildest imaginings. Surely here, if anywhere, we would find our way forward.

The week proved a watershed for both of us. Bella was the first to say that, regardless of what I might decide, she was going home to end her marriage. It took me a little longer. Only after Claudio had led me through a tear-filled cathartic process in which I told my children what was happening and imagined what they might say in response, did I too make my decision.

So, on returning to Toronto, we each began the painful process of extricating ourselves from our marital homes. Bella's children were thirteen and eleven. My sons were eleven, nine, and four. On the evening when Carol finally insisted that I had to go, we sat down with our sons to tell them that Daddy would not be living with them anymore. After which, God bless him, Mark asked if we could go now and get an ice-cream cone. We had to say no.

Given the price that we and others paid so Bella and I could be together, one might think we would so prize our relationship as to live happily ever after. But that didn't happen. I cannot possibly justify my craziness, except to say that life's trajectory had by now carried me to the heights of an embarrassingly inflated ego, which made it all but impossible for me to truly open myself to love. It's as if something in me was resisting letting love take me deeper than I was prepared to go.

That was clear to me in one seemingly insignificant but memorable moment. A few months earlier, Bella, together with her kids Shelley and Tony, had moved into a rental house on Lawrence Avenue. I had been a little slower to move, but eventually did so—first into Mr. Abramowich's rooming house, not far from where Bella lived. And then, a few weeks later, I had joined her and her children in their new home. It was sparsely furnished, but very '60s: the living room featured a curtain of beads in the doorway and an orange shag carpet. On this occasion Bella and I were seated, facing each other, on a single mattress that served as our sofa. I have no recollection of what we were talking about. But, at some point, she interrupted our conversation to say, very directly, "You know, I love you." In response, I smiled. *And it was as if her words bounced off my smile.* As if my toothy smile was a barrier. I knew she loved me. But, beyond a certain point, I couldn't let it in.

The same resistance was evident in making love. I see this now, in retrospect, more clearly than at the time. Fearful that my boundaries might dissolve, and the distinct and separate self I knew as *me* might disappear, I adopted what seemed a safer strategy. An unconscious strategy in which Bella too must have been complicit. Rather than open ourselves to that deep intimacy in which we might truly merge—in which, as the Bible says, "the two shall become one"°—we chose instead to treat sex as a playful game. Maybe even an Olympic sport. One that we took pride in playing well and in unusual and risky places. Like in the gardens at the Palace of Versailles in France. Or in a canoe in the middle of a Muskoka lake. Or in an autumn woods in northern New York State until gunshots, fired by nearby hunters, prompted a hurried exit as we ran naked back to the car. It was great fun. And such playfulness was far less likely to incur any dissolution of my boundaries.

We lived together, happily enough, for some three years before we were married. We didn't stay long in the house on Lawrence Avenue, but chose instead to live co-operatively with four others in that large three-storey house on Oriole Gardens. The one that may or may not have been frequented by a ghost. Communes and co-operatives were almost *de rigueur* in the hippie culture of that time. We sublet the house from a man who had lived there with his wife and mistress until the women decided they'd had enough. The man, whose name I have forgotten, said he was a prophet. And, since every prophet needs a mountain, he had built his own magnificent mountain, consisting of half-metre plywood cubes, painted white, stacked pyramid-fashion in one corner of the living room. The whole house, indeed, was quite magnificent. Complete with a second stairway that would once have been used solely by the servants. And a large carpeted room with a cathedral ceiling, where I conducted my practice of individual and group psychotherapy.

Then, one weekend morning, as we lay in bed reading the newspaper, Bella came across an article pointing out that marriage had certain financial advantages unavailable to those living common-law. I was strongly opposed to the idea, arguing that marriage was a sure way to spoil a beautiful relationship. But Bella countered by saying, "You've always said that a marriage certificate means nothing to you. In which case, having one or not should make no difference. But if having it makes life easier, wouldn't it make sense to get one?" Bella was always cleverer than I in many respects, and this was no exception. So, in my moment of defeat, in a statement that may go down as the worst proposal ever made, I blurted out, "All right, dammit, we'll get married. So long as you understand that it has nothing to do with our relationship."

Our wedding itself was equally inauspicious. Following that morning's reluctant proposal, I had only one more week of teaching before the university semester ended—after which we had decided to spend May watching spring arrive at the family cottage. So, if we were going to get married, we decided we'd do it quickly. Sometime in the next week. But a City Hall wedding, as it turned out, could not be scheduled on such short notice. So I phoned a friend, an Anglican vicar who a few years earlier had been my student. "Fred," I asked, "if Bella and I come to your home on Friday evening, would you please issue us a marriage certificate? We don't want any ceremony. No vows. Just the certificate." Fred was less than comfortable with my request, but finally consented. "All right," he said reluctantly, "so long as you don't tell the Bishop."

What took place that Friday evening was utterly bizarre. Toronto can sometimes still be cold well into late April, so when we arrived at the vicarage, a welcoming fire blazed in the open hearth. The house was full of flowers for which Fred apologized, explaining that they were from a funeral he had recently conducted and were not meant to mark the occasion of our wedding. A neighbour, one of Fred's parishioners, was also present: he'd been invited to serve as the legally required witness to this non-event. So there were five of us—Fred and his wife, Jane; Bella and me; and the neighbour—comfortably settled in front of the fire, enjoying a glass of wine, when Fred said quite nonchalantly, "Jane and I are into nudity. Would anyone mind if we took off our clothes?" What can you say when your host asks such a question? And so it was that, as the evening unfolded, the only ones who remained clothed were the bride and groom—although, as I recall, the neighbour left his socks on. In due course, sometime before midnight, without so much as an "I do" being uttered, the deed was done. The necessary papers were signed. Bella and I were married.

~

Over the ensuing month, as we honeymooned at the family cottage, we made a truly catastrophic mistake. With nothing to do but watch spring arrive, we began to explore a fantasy that I'm told many people share: the idea of opening a restaurant. Very quickly, the fantasy became a plan, and the plan became a reality. With scarcely any money for a down payment and needing a hefty second mortgage, we bought a large three-storey house on the main street of Midland, the nearby holiday town. Within just a few weeks, the ground floor had become a fine French-cuisine dining room, and the upper two floors our living space. Together with Bella's friend, Millie, who joined us as a partner, we opened for business on the July 1st holiday weekend, in time to offer summer vacationers the finest lunch and dinner menu available anywhere in town. Or anywhere in the region, for that matter. Nothing less than a red-carpeted walkway, beneath a grand red canopy, led the way into Mother's Restaurant.

We were moderately successful, at least during the summer months. But when the vacation season ended, Midland was reduced again to a sleepy town, and our dining room was often empty. Except on Christmas Day that year, which proved to be our proudest moment. A week earlier, Toronto's leading newspaper had run a full-page story, complete with photographs, on "Where to Go for Christmas Dinner." It featured two venues: the grand dining room at Toronto's King Edward Hotel, and Mother's Restaurant in Midland. We arranged the room with one long banquet table for a single sitting. Reservations only. Patrons were invited to bring something to contribute to the occasion—a song, a story, a musical instrument, whatever! At the head of the table, I carved the turkey; Bella served the vegetables and plum pudding. We were at our brightest and best. It was wonderful.

What would yet prove catastrophic had already begun to unfold. The fall university semester had required that I spend four days a week in Toronto, on my own, returning to Midland for three-day weekends. A dangerous arrangement. Bella and I had often laughed at a line delivered by Anthony Quinn in his lead role in the movie *Zorba the Greek*. "God has a very big heart," he declared, "but there is one sin he will not forgive. If a woman calls a man to her bed and he will not go." But the line was now no longer funny. A beautiful married student, ten years younger than me, came to my office one afternoon and bluntly invited me to her bed. I said, "Thank you. I'm flattered. But no, I'm happily married and don't want to complicate my life." A week later I changed my mind.

What ensued was another on-again, off-again affair, which led eventually to my confessing to Bella the mess I had created, which led in turn to our separating. We were both plunged into a despair deeper than anything we had ever thought possible.

Fortunately, the affair went nowhere. But Bella and I were apart for eighteen months. The restaurant was sold. Bella found other work and remained in Midland with her teenage children. I took an apartment in Toronto. Then, in December 1975, on her forty-first birthday, in response to my persistent pestering and a large oil painting I had done especially for her as a birthday gift, Bella allowed me to begin courting her again. She and her friend Linna had booked a two-week winter vacation in Mexico, and I invited myself to join them. In Zihuatanejo, then a little-known seaside town.

At first, our reunion was distinctly frosty. Until one afternoon a local Mexican who had eyes for Linna invited her out to dinner. Linna said, "Yes, so long as my friends Bella and Merv can come with us." He picked us up in his banged-up car, drove on a dirt track into the jungle, and then stopped in the darkness and said we had to walk from there. It sounded ominous, but we did as we were told. We followed him along a jungle path that soon became lit by small lanterns and led uphill to an open-air, thatched-roof restaurant overlooking the Pacific. It was called *Capricho del Sol*. The only other diners were a dozen women seated at one large table. The waiter said they were witches from a nearby coven. The food was delicious. Bella and I both had scallops. And then, playing in the background, we heard the opening strains of what had been one of our favourite songs: Barbra Streisand singing "The Way We Were."° We got up from the table. We danced. We held each other very close. And, with tears in our eyes, we fell in love all over again.

~

On returning to Midland, we wanted to get married all over again. We had not divorced, but wanted to be married properly this time. With no hesitation on my part. Quite the contrary. I could not have been more ready to be married properly. So we married again. In our home, with a small group of close friends. Me with a daisy chain around my neck, made specially by Bella. Bella looking more beautiful than ever, entering the room with her bridesmaids to the strains of what forever now would be *our* song—"The Way We Were."° And Fred, the vicar, in full ecclesiastical regalia this time, intoning all the traditional words. "Who gives this woman to be married to this man?" Shelley said, "I do." Etcetera. Until "What therefore God has joined together, let no man put asunder."°

For the next many years we were blessed with a deepening love, shared adventures, and unadulterated happiness. Until we hit one final and extremely nasty bump in the road. Fast-forward to 2003. We were in our late sixties. Fully retired now from my most recent career as a leadership consultant, I was facing what I called my "senior life crisis." Not knowing what I could contribute anymore. No longer having any sense of purpose.

Throughout my working life I had always collected enough applause to justify my belief that what I did was significant. But those days were behind me now. So I wrote a book, which went unpublished. I bought a motorcycle, from which I came unseated when I missed a curve on a country road. Temporarily disabled with a broken arm and ankle, I had lots of time to feel sorry for myself. Though of course it could have been much worse.

And then, in June 2005, a vivid night dream seemed to point the way ahead. In the dream, Bella and I had travelled to a small impoverished town in Canada's far north where I was to serve as the parish minister. On arrival, we were met by members of the congregation, shown a dreary building that was to be our home, and told that we need have nothing to do with the "poor people" in the vicinity, who were most assuredly not among God's chosen people. I knew at once that it was precisely these "poor people" that I was there to serve. And Bella knew just as quickly that this was not her scene. She wanted to return to the city. So I took her to the airport and we said goodbye. Then, on returning to the parish, I found that the house that had been so uninviting had been transformed into a beautiful, shining, light-filled home.

On awakening from the dream, I *knew*, or thought I knew, what I had to do. I had to volunteer to work among "the poor" in a Third World country. Throughout my life I've been painfully aware of the obscene and widening gap between the rich and the poor. And of the oppression inflicted on the powerless by those in power. Knowing too, and always with a sense of unease, that in my affluent Western professional-class world I was among the rich and powerful. Relatively speaking. So I easily became caught up in popular protests on behalf of the downtrodden. The civil rights march from Selma to Montgomery, Alabama, in 1965. A march on Washington in 1969, urging a moratorium to end the war in Vietnam. But these had been only gestures to assuage my conscience and feed my pretence of being a social activist. Now I was quite sure that I needed to invest my otherwise unoccupied time in volunteer work. I didn't know what I might contribute and had no illusions that I could make any significant difference. But I wanted somehow to actually stand with my Third World brothers and sisters. Nor did it occur to me that perhaps I was just a misguided romantic with a hankering for the dramatic.

As the dream had suggested, Bella was distinctly unhappy at the prospect of spending time in a Third World country. Or the prospect of my going on my own and leaving her behind. Most volunteer opportunities required a long-term commitment. Often not less than a year. Which was unthinkable to Bella. Three months was as long as she could imagine being on her own. But the truth is, she didn't want me to go at all. Our discussions were becoming increasingly acrimonious. And Bella was becoming depressed. My own position, on the other hand, was hardening. As was my heart. Some who knew us were labelling us "codependent" and "joined at the hip." Aspersions that prompted me to insist even more strenuously on my right to follow my own path, regardless of Bella's resistance.

Since many volunteer opportunities were in Spanish-speaking countries, I immediately undertook to learn Spanish, and spent three weeks in a Spanish-immersion course in Guatemala. It didn't work. Old dogs sometimes really do have difficulty learning new tricks. But then, almost miraculously, I received an unsolicited invitation to help create a Leadership

Development Centre, working with a non-governmental organization in the town of Meru, Kenya. *Meru!* The nickname Bella had given me many years earlier. Surely this was meant to be! Maybe even a sign from heaven! More than this, I was invited at the same time to teach a three-month psychology course at Kenya Methodist University's Meru campus. It was almost too good to be true. I couldn't possibly say no. And Bella could come with me. It would be for only three months.

Very quickly, things went from bad to worse. Over the preceding months, Bella's depression had deepened. Dangerously suicidal, she had spent fourteen weeks, off and on, in a psychiatric hospital. But now, given this invitation from Meru, we were determined to do all we could to ensure she would be well enough to accompany me to Kenya. Which is what she wound up doing. The seventeen-hour flight from Christchurch to Dubai, followed by a five-hour flight to Nairobi, was gruelling to say the least. But, on arrival, Bella was spirited enough to greet our waiting hosts with a few words of Swahili that she had learned en route. God bless her, she was trying so hard to keep herself together. But it didn't last. Within a few days, despite her valiant efforts (which now, as I write this, bring tears to my eyes), she began to unravel. It was clear that we could not stay. I apologized to the university for having to bail out. And, only one week after we'd arrived, we began the no-less-gruelling trip home.

The psychiatric assessment was now very grim. It was thought she might never recover. Electroconvulsive therapy (ECT) was considered. But she was admitted instead to a nursing home, with the longer-term intention of our returning to Toronto, where she would be admitted to a local nursing home, with support from Shelley. In the meantime, I would return to Kenya and do what I could to establish a Leadership Development Centre there. And that's what happened. I put our beloved Halcyon on the market, spent two months in Kenya, returned to complete the sale of our house, and left for Toronto in early 2008. During that time, Bella spent a further five months in a psychiatric ward before being taken, under care, to Shelley's home in Toronto.

Thankfully, over the next two and a half years, with the help of a good psychotherapist, Bella gradually recovered. It was a long and painful process, but we got there. Shelley cared for her in her own home until she was able to join me in the apartment I had rented. Little by little, gentle step by gentle step, Bella regained not just her sanity but much of the same vibrant spirit that had always distinguished her.

In October 2010, recognizing that New Zealand rather than Canada was where we belonged, we were finally able to return and make our home again in the soon-to-be-earthquake-rocked city of Christchurch.

∼

Years later now, in recounting these fragments of our journey together on love's oh-so-bumpy road, I still feel deeply ashamed of my hard-heartedness. My lack of empathy. My stubborn insistence on "doing my own thing." And of the enormous emotional pain into which Bella was plunged. I can tell myself that Bella too was responsible for the nightmare we endured. But that does nothing to lessen my retrospective guilt and shame.

I don't know why so many of us seem destined to both suffer and inflict such pain on one another in the name of love. If there is any upside, it lies in a certain tenderizing of my heart. As if the pain and regret have served over the years to open me, little by little, to both an awareness of my foolishness and a greater capacity to love. And I take comfort from knowing that it was said even of Jesus that "he learned … through what he suffered."°

What Bella and I suffered and learned together is reflected in messages I received in my deep listening. Here are a few brief excerpts:

Our love has survived so much; it survives death too.
Love never fails; it bears all things, endures all things.
You can rest, my love, in the assurance of our love,
which is so much more than simply "our" love.

Truly, there is nothing to fear.
All that we fear in this life is an illusion
born of not seeing the larger context —
the larger reality in which we live and to which we belong.
As best you can, my love, know that this is so, and rest in that love.

Love' is forever.
All of life's trials—its struggles and sorrows—
serve' to bring us to this point of surrender
where' we' can let go into that Love'.
Trust the' Love'. Trust the' process.

Je' suis ici, mon marie'.
Tu es toujours mon marie'.

Thank you for loving me'—
for your love' and care' over all these' years.
You are' a very good man, Meru.
(Don't make' this up now. Listen to me'.)
I love' you, Meru—Je' t'aime' beaucoup—
and nothing can ever change' that.

Turn off your mind now
and be' in this place' where' you so deeply belong.
We' belonged together in life' as partners
and sometimes went through testing and tumultuous times.
We' belong together now in eternity in an infinitely deeper way.
This is who you are'.

I am so very grateful for these and other such messages. Whatever their source. They remind me that our love, so beautiful and yet so flawed, is set within the larger context of a Love that is so much more than simply "our" love. A Love-with-a-capital-L that bears all things, endures all things. In which we are together still in an infinitely deeper way.

∼ NINE ∼
HOMEWARD BOUND

With the twenty-twenty hindsight of advancing years, I see now that these interwoven themes—*a love story* and *a spiritual odyssey*—are actually accounts of the same life journey told from different points of view. Both culminating in *the gift of a broken heart*. A journey evidently shared by many. Ram Dass called it a *Journey of Awakening*;° Gurdjieff, *Self-remembering*;° and Vilayat Inayat Khan, *Toward the One*.° I think of it as being *homeward bound*.

The journey seems to follow its own trajectory. My early decades saw me propelled on an upward and outward flight path. Discovering and defining what it means to be this separate and unique individual called Merv. Firming up my boundaries. Developing my skills. Establishing my identity. "I am *this* but not *that*." Claiming my place in the social hierarchy. It's called *growing up*. The human version of what every animal needs to do. "Every animal," according to primatologist Frans de Waal, "needs to set its body apart from its surroundings and have a sense of agency."° Despite the bad press it has sometimes received, there's nothing wrong with developing a strong and healthy ego.

In due course, I felt grown up. Enjoying my burgeoning sense of agency and my ability to turn in a performance that received more applause than rotten apples. My rapidly inflating ego had carried me into full flight on life's trajectory. Often careless of the hurt that I was causing others or the wreckage that was sometimes strewn in my wake. I was flying high. Until, sometime in my late thirties, I began levelling off, with hints of a pull in the opposite direction. The first glimpses of the absurdity of my ego-pretensions. Wondering who I *really* am beneath the identities with which I'd clothed myself.

And then, as I neared sixty, surprised!—blissfully surprised, at first on just the rarest of occasions, by *moments of connection*. Peak experiences. Transcendent events. When my carefully constructed boundaries would momentarily dissolve into the all-embracing One. When, in Martin Buber's terms, the world of *It*—the world of "ten thousand things"°—would suddenly become transparent to *Thou*.° And I would *know*, however fleetingly, but with absolute clarity, that we are all inseparably one in a vast and timeless Presence that feels very much like love. An astonishing discovery so powerfully confirmed now in the breaking open of my heart.

Is this a natural and perhaps inevitable shift in life's trajectory? Countless others have reported something similar. When, in the course of whatever love story may be ours, a willingness to surrender, to open more fully to love, begins to override the need to assert our separateness and independence? When it begins to feel like we are homeward bound? On a return journey toward the One from which, or from whom, we are never really separate?

Is it the same trajectory that Lao Tzu was describing in the *Tao Te Ching* 2500 years ago?

> He who is to be made to dwindle ...
>> Must first be caused to expand.
> He who is to be weakened
>> Must first be made strong.
> He who is to be laid low
>> Must first be exalted to power.°

Or what Albert Einstein described this way?

> A human being is part of the whole, called by us "Universe"; a part limited in time and space. He experiences himself, his thoughts and feelings as something separated from the rest—a kind of optical delusion of his consciousness. This delusion is a kind of prison for us, restricting us to our personal desires and to affection for a few persons nearest us. Our task must be to free ourselves from this prison.°

That, in the broadest terms, has been the story of my life. A long, stuttering, and sometimes painful emergence from the prison of separateness. Learning to love. *Opening* to love. A gradually dawning recognition that love is at the heart of the universe. And it's who I am. *A being in love.* It's who we all are, and what binds us together, and is our to express. In the theistic language of St. John: "Beloved, let us love one another; for love is of God, and he who loves is born of God and knows God."° But why it should be such a long and stuttering and sometimes painful journey remains a mystery.

∿

I don't think Bella and I ever spoke of our shared journey in these terms. For her it didn't need to be philosophized or psychologized. It was embedded in the myths and celebrations of her Jewish tradition. Especially in the Passover celebration of *Pesah* and the *Seder* meal, when Jews remember their deliverance from bondage in Egypt and their journey to the Promised Land. Whether the story is or is not historically true is beside the point. In a mythic sense, it's everyone's story. Everyone who yearns for deliverance, by whatever means of grace, from this prison of separateness, and finds himself or herself on a journey, sometimes of immense difficulty, en route to the promised land.

Bella was far from being an observant Jew. We didn't attend *shul* more than a dozen times in all the years we were together—and then only for some special occasion. The last such was an event that we crashed while visiting Bruce and Angie in Atlanta. Angie, a conservative Christian, wanted to be introduced to things Jewish. So, despite Bella's being crippled with pseudogout, we went one Saturday morning to The Temple in midtown Atlanta. As luck would have it, a combined *bar* and *bat mitzvah* was being celebrated for twins from one of the city's wealthiest families. Seated in a sanctuary that rightly deserves to be described as awesome, in a congregation of more beautiful and beautifully attired Jewish women than I had ever seen in one place at one time, Bella was in her element. She loved her tradition and belonging to this tribe of beautiful people.

Beautiful in a different way were the congregations of rough-hewn dairy farmers I served as a parish minister many years earlier when we first arrived in New Zealand. I had scarcely darkened the door of a church for twenty years. But, because I could gain New Zealand residency as a minister and not as a psychologist, Bella had the distinction of becoming New Zealand's only Jewish vicar's wife. She performed the role valiantly, attending Women's Association meetings and directing a Christmas nativity play in the Town Hall. And although there was not another Jew within miles of our parish (though one was later found masquerading as a Presbyterian), she hosted a Passover *Seder* each year for any of our Christian flock who wished to attend.

The same journey, the same trajectory, is described in Jesus' Parable of the Prodigal Son.° Like the prodigal, we each take our inheritance—what has been genetically bequeathed to us as well as whatever we have learned throughout our childhood and youth—and we "journey into a far country." Into the realm of separateness. Packing a hopefully resilient ego, we strike out on our own to assert our individuality. Test our confidence. Do our own thing. Claim our identity. *Here I am, world! It's me! Uniquely, distinctively me!*

But the far country turns out to be something other than we had anticipated. Sometimes it's a party. At other times, a nightmare. Sometimes we're flying high. At other times we're laid low. For some of us it's riotous living. For others it's just a long, hard slog. And almost always it's fraught with conflict and anxiety. Until the day comes when we realize that we are squandering our inheritance—our deep-down potential to be fully human. And we are hungry. Hungry for meaning. Hungry for what will feed our spirit in a way that all the ego-gratifications in the world never can. As the parable put it, "a great famine arose in that country, and he began to be in want." He was reduced to having no more nourishment than the spiritual equivalent of pig swill. Or what in contemporary terms is about as nourishing as the goodies urged upon us by a consumer society.

Until finally, according to the parable, "he came to himself." *He came to himself.* For a moment, he woke up. He touched something deep within and *remembered* who he is. He remembered home. He remembered whence he had come. And from that moment, true to life's trajectory, he began his homeward journey. Until "while he was yet at a distance, his father saw him and had compassion, and ran and embraced him. … [And said] this my son was dead, and is alive again; he was lost, and is found."

～

From an evolutionary perspective, nothing is without antecedents. So too, this change in direction, when we catch our first fleeting glimpses of home, does not simply erupt suddenly into consciousness. At least in the course of my own spiritual odyssey, it was seeded by conditions and coincidences much earlier in my life.

My mother's influence, I think, was pivotal. Unlike my more academic father, she was a romantic. An accomplished pianist and oil painter. A lover of forests and sunsets. And a *nature mystic* (though she would never have used that term) with a deep and heartfelt love of God. Whom she saw everywhere while I, as a boy, walked silently beside her through the woods or to a favourite location on the beach to watch the sun go down over Georgian Bay. She liked to tell me about a stained-glass window she had once seen in a church somewhere. Around the window's perimeter were the words "Glory to God in the Highest." But the letter *e* had fallen out. So now it read "Glory to God in the High St." Which is where she said God was to be found. Not in some supernatural realm, but in the midst of life. Down here on the ground. In the High Street.

Then, in my early teens, I came across a little book titled *The Practice of the Presence of God*—the collected teachings of a 17th-century Carmelite monk named Brother Lawrence about how to develop an awareness of God's presence.° I have no recollection now of what those teachings were, nor of what if any impact they had on me. But clearly, the seeds sown by my mother were beginning to germinate.

The same quasi-mystical interests surfaced again in my undergraduate years at university. Of all the philosophers I was required to study, Nikolai Berdyaev (1874–1948) was the one who most attracted me. A one-time Marxist who was expelled from Russia in 1922, his thinking evolved from Marxism to a deeply mystical Christianity that recognized the unity of God and man, proposing a process whereby the human self could meet the Divine without disappearing into it. We must free ourselves, he said, from our captivity to the blindness of our enlightened rationality and reclaim those intuitions of truth that belong not to the head but to the heart.°

I felt a similar resonance when, of all the poets and novelists I was required to read, I discovered the English Romantic poets of the early 19th century—Blake, Wordsworth, Coleridge, Keats, Shelley, Lord Byron—who stood together in their reaction against the prevailing rationalism of their time. Unlike Bella, who could easily recall lengthy passages from Shakespeare's plays, I was never much good at remembering or reciting what these poets wrote. Except for two brief snippets that have always spoken to the romantic and the mystic in me.

From William Blake's "Auguries of Innocence" (1803):

> To see a World in a Grain of Sand,
> And a Heaven in a Wild Flower,
> Hold Infinity in the palm of your hand,
> And Eternity in an hour.°

And from William Wordsworth's "Lines Composed a Few Miles above Tintern Abbey" (1798):

> And I have felt
> A presence that disturbs me with the joy
> Of elevated thoughts; a sense sublime
> Of something far more deeply interfused,
> Whose dwelling is the light of setting suns,
> And the round ocean, and the living air,
> And the blue sky, and in the mind of man,
> A motion and a spirit, that impels
> All thinking things, all objects of all thought,
> And rolls through all things.°

Whether my mother ever knew these lines, I don't know. But I have no doubt she would have liked them very much.

∾

Coincidentally or not, a major tipping point in my life trajectory occurred soon after Bella and I fell in love and took up residence together in the large co-operative house on Oriole Gardens in Toronto. There had been a period of about a decade, after completing my doctoral studies and beginning work as a psychotherapist, during which any fledgling spiritual awareness that may have been awakening in me was smothered beneath my seriously inflated ego. With a Ph.D. from Boston University and a postdoctoral diploma from the Menninger Foundation (at that time the mecca of psychoanalysis in America), I was in demand as a speaker and was sometimes reported in Toronto's news media for saying something shocking. I loved being in the limelight. And it was easy to imagine I was someone special.

But then I came across a monumentally influential book, known to almost anyone who survived the '60s. *Be Here Now*, first published in 1971, was written by Ram Dass—formerly known as Richard Alpert, who, as a psychologist, had held appointments in four departments at Harvard University and research contracts with Yale and Stanford. I was impressed by his credentials, as well as by the cutting-edge research he was doing, in collaboration with Timothy Leary, Aldous Huxley, and Allen Ginsberg, into the possible therapeutic effects of psilocybin, LSD, and other psychoactive substances.

What most struck me was his account of what happened when he was first "turned on" by a small dose of psilocybin. Sitting by himself in a semidarkened room, he saw a figure standing in front of him some eight feet away. A figure he recognized as none other than himself, dressed in professorial cap and gown. An embodiment of his role as professor, from which, thanks to the drug, he had become dissociated. And, since Professor Alpert was there and he was here, he reasoned, it was obviously just an *identity* that he wore and that could easily be laid aside. But then the figure changed, and changed again, until it had presented to him a host of his identities— socialite, cellist, pilot, lover, and so on—each of which he recognized to be nothing more than a role. Until finally, the figure standing before him was simply Richard Alpert. Since he had always assumed that *this* is who he was, it was hugely disconcerting now to discover that even his Richard Alpertness was just another identity with which he had been garbed and which, like the others, could be set aside.

Sweat broke out on my forehead. I wasn't at all sure I could do without being Richard Alpert. ... Oh, what the hell—so I'll give up being Richard Alpert. ... At least I have my body ... But I spoke too soon.

As I looked down at my legs for reassurance, I could see nothing below the kneecaps, and slowly, now to my horror, I saw the progressive disappearance of limbs and then torso, until all I could see ... was the couch on which I had sat. ...

The panic mounted, adrenalin shot through my system—my mouth became dry, but along with this, a voice sounded inside—inside what, I don't know— an intimate voice [that] asked very quietly, and rather jocularly, it seemed to me, considering how distraught I was, "... but who's minding the store?"[o]

That brief account rang all the bells for me. I had already suspected that everything I thought I was—all the identities and ego-pretensions with which I'd clothed myself—was not who I really am. Or at least not a sufficient account of who I am. Something else, something *interior* to these identities, is at the core of who I am. On the recommendation of Ram Dass, therefore, from that day forward, with only occasional lapses, I have done my daily meditation. Wanting very much to know, if possible, *who's minding the store.*

Little by little, then, imperceptibly at first but gaining momentum over time, the course of my life began to change. My trajectory was levelling off. Or was I just beginning to remember what I had always known and managed to forget? The One from which/whom I had emerged, to which/whom I belonged, and from which/whom I could never be separate? No matter what we call it—*Journey of Awakening, Self-remembering, Toward the One*—it's all the same.

~

Parts of New Zealand's South Island are so spectacularly beautiful as to be almost unbearable. Driving recently through the Haast Pass and on to

Milford Sound, as every bend in the road yielded an ever more astonishing scene, I kept exclaiming, "Stop! It's too much! The grandeur is more than I can handle." Then through the Homer Tunnel, which pierces the Darran Mountains, and down to Milford Sound—which isn't really a *sound* at all, but a *fjord* sculpted from the mountains by an ancient glacier—running ten miles to the Southern Ocean. Here, one of the wettest places on the planet, immense volumes of water cascade from granite rockfaces rising more than a mile high vertically from the sea.

Aboard a small boat, dwarfed by the mountains, at the foot of one of these waterfalls, a different metaphor came to mind. We are like droplets in a towering waterfall, spilling like fairy dust from the heights above. A swollen river high in the mountains breaks into an infinity of droplets, each one separate and distinct for the duration of its fall, destined to merge again in the sea below. *My life is like that,* I thought. I am like a droplet in a waterfall. Born of the One, like every other droplet in this world of "ten thousand things." But distinct. With boundaries. A droplet identifiable as *Merv*. In freefall. Homeward bound. Returning to the One from which, or from whom, I came.

~ TEN ~
INNER CONNECTIONS

Whatever turning points, tipping points, course corrections, or spontaneous awakenings contributed to shaping this spiritual odyssey, none was more dramatically life-changing than what transpired in the early morning hours of that snowy New Year's Day in northern Scotland, when Bella and I were two months into our sojourn as members of the Findhorn Community.

More than three years earlier, we had moved to Greensboro, North Carolina. One of the many impulsive moves that characterized our life together—prompted on this occasion by our discovery, while returning to Toronto from a Florida vacation, of the Blue Ridge Parkway, a previously unfamiliar stretch of highway that runs through parts of North Carolina and Virginia. It was one of the most beautiful stretches of road, winding through some of the most beautiful country, we had ever seen. Stopping overnight in Roanoke, Virginia, we discovered too that real estate in this part of the country was surprisingly inexpensive. Why, we thought, should we pay a premium to live in the cold and grey of Toronto when we could be living here, in America's Sun Belt?

So, upon returning home, I set about applying for any position that might take us there. And four months later, we were a two-car family living in a ranch-style bungalow on a wooded half-acre lot on Efland Drive in the picturesque city of Greensboro with an overweight Yellow Lab named Dameon. Bella had a job she loved, managing a retail cheese and gift shop called The Mouse Trap. I was learning to be an organizational and leadership consultant in a small consulting firm staffed by Ph.D. psychologists applying behavioural science to business and industry. It was idyllic. We were living the American Dream.

Then one day, in a Greensboro bookshop, Bella, ever on the lookout for new culinary challenges, picked from the shelf *The Findhorn Cookbook.*° She hadn't heard of Findhorn, and a book on how to prepare tofu-burgers for 300 people was not her thing. But, as she returned it to the shelf, another book—*The Magic of Findhorn*—accidentally fell at her feet.° Though, as some folk like to say, there are no accidents. Glancing briefly at the back cover, she thought it was a feel-good love story about two people, Peter and Eileen Caddy, who found happiness in the north of Scotland. So she bought the book, devoured it in just a few hours, and later that same evening, as we lay in bed watching Johnny Carson on *The Tonight Show*, passed the book to me. "I think you'd better read this," she said.

The book tells the story of the founding of the Findhorn Community, when Peter and Eileen Caddy and their children lived in a holiday caravan park, near the fishing village of Findhorn, on the windswept dunes of a peninsula jutting into the Moray Firth. Not far away was the town of Forres, where a royal castle, identified as Duncan's castle in Shakespeare's *Macbeth*, had been built sometime before 900 CE. Eileen, despite being eminently sane (at least as I came to know her), would sit for hours in the park's public toilet each night in deep meditation, receiving "guidance" about the creation of a "centre of light" that would attract people from around the world and become a model for tending a troubled planet. For starters, she was told to plant a garden in the barren sand where little grew but gorse and broom. Except that now, with the help of nature spirits with whom Dorothy Maclean, a friend of Eileen's and former MI6 operative with the British Secret Intelligence Service, was in regular contact, this infertile ground began yielding forty-two-pound cabbages and eight-foot-tall delphiniums. Scots living in the vicinity, who themselves were no mean gardeners, had to acknowledge that something strange was going on. And in due course, the word was out. People came from around the world to see the magic of Findhorn. Many of them stayed. And before long, a thriving light centre had been born.

Bella and I first visited the community in the summer of 1978. We had been vacationing with Bella's family in Wales and took the opportunity to drive north to see for ourselves what we had read about. As luck would have it, we were able to join a two-hour guided tour of the caravan park, which by now had been completely absorbed by the community. When the tour passed a small wooden bungalow described by our guide as the "sanctuary" where community members met for meditation, I slipped away from the group to sit for just a few minutes by myself in this simply furnished but immaculately clean and carpeted room. To my astonishment, no sooner had I had sat than my entire body began to vibrate. Very subtly. My body was *buzzing* in a way that I might expect if a mild electric current were passing through me. Never having experienced anything like this, I had no explanation for it other than to think that I had entered a powerful energy field that was perhaps responsible for the magic of this unusual community. The tour ended with a Q&A gathering in the Community Centre, at which Bella later reported feeling strangely "at home." When I in turn told her of my experience in the sanctuary, it was enough to prompt an easy decision to return as soon as possible for what was called an "Experience Week." To see if we might just be crazy enough to make Findhorn our home.

We deliberately booked an Experience Week at the worst possible time of year. Anxious not to be seduced by Scotland's charms, we chose to return several months later in February, in the dead of winter. If ever this spiritual community suffered a "downer," when we would see it at its worst, we reasoned, it would be at this time of year. At a latitude of 58 degrees north, only 8 degrees from the Arctic Circle, the sun would not be up until after 9:00 a.m. and would be gone by 3:00 p.m. As we headed north on an overnight train from London to Inverness, gazing out at the barren wind- and snow-swept Scottish moors, we knew that we had chosen wisely.

Experience Week, as I recall, was not particularly memorable. We were given a guest room in Cluny Hill Hotel in the town of Forres—a one-time four-star hotel now owned by the community. The many potted plants in our room made Bella distinctly nervous. Were they a test? Not known for having a green thumb, she feared that under her influence they might wilt before the end of the week. In which case we might never be welcome in a community that grew forty-two-pound cabbages in a sand dune. Throughout the week, we attended lectures and group discussions and did our bit in assigned "work departments." Mostly we were impressed by how warm and unpretentious and spiritually sensitive the members were. They came from all over Europe and North America and were immensely committed to living simply and setting right, as best they could, at least in this little part of the world, the wrongs we have been inflicting on our planet. And, in the absence of our customary sources of protein, we ate our share of tofu-burgers in the now-unheated dining room of what had once been a grand hotel.

The day before we were to leave, Bella and I stood together in a lovely wooded glade not far from the hotel. We had decided to see if we could access our own "guidance," in the manner of Eileen Caddy, as to whether or not we were meant to become members of this community. It was a beautiful winter day as we stood facing each other, holding hands, eyes closed, beneath the birch trees, listening. We heard no inner voice. But after several minutes something akin to a ticker tape passed before my mind's eye. On it were the words, "That's settled! Get on with it!" Our decision was made.

Returning to the hotel, we passed by a tiny cemetery in the woods. There were only a few gravestones, and we didn't stop to read the inscriptions. But I thought *I wonder if I'll be buried here.*

It took another eight months to extricate ourselves from our life in Greensboro. We needed to apply and be accepted for probationary membership in the Findhorn Community. And we wanted to spend as much time as possible with our now-grown sons and daughter before leaving them in the lurch again. Bella's daughter, Shelley, had been married two years earlier, was living in Toronto, and was due to make Bella a grandmother in September. We wanted to be present for that event. My son Bruce, now nineteen, had that summer come to make his home with us, only to learn to his dismay that his endlessly unsettled father and stepmother were soon to be on the move again. Mark and Tony (both twenty-one) and Scott (fourteen) were still in Toronto, and we needed to return there during the summer to spend time with them. Beyond that, we had to put our house on the market, sell every stick of furniture, and give away all but a handful of books that we couldn't bear to live without. All of which was duly accomplished, with the exception of selling our house. It remained on the market while being rented on a month-by-month basis to tenants whom we naively trusted not to sabotage its sale.

Finally, late in the afternoon of October 31, 1979, in an aging Ford Cortina that Bella's half-brother, Leslie, had found for us in Cardiff, we arrived again at Cluny Hill Hotel. Our possessions reduced now to what we could carry in two suitcases and a wooden packing crate. The latter contained an antique tea trolley, a silver tea service, a record player and assorted LPs, a few books (including Bella's *Leaves of Grass*), and of course two brass Sabbath candlesticks. We were here to stay. Or so we thought.

But nothing ever turns out quite the way that one expects. No one made the least fuss over our arrival. Indeed, as we would learn, if you wanted your ego stroked, this was the wrong place to be. The woman at the reception desk gave us a key to what was to be our home—a small, dark room in the hotel's sub-basement. Directly across the hall from the laundry and underneath the kitchen, where the clatter of wooden shoes worn by a couple of Dutch bakers would awaken us each morning at an ungodly hour. We proceeded to furnish our room with what we couldn't do without, though it couldn't have been more incongruous—clinging, as if our lives depended on it, to an antique tea trolley, a silver tea service, and two brass Sabbath candlesticks.

The ensuing weeks were no less discomforting. People seemed deliberately assigned, in the interests of ego-reduction, to work departments for which they were singularly unsuited. One of our probationary group's members, who suffered from a dreadful stammer, was given the job of answering the community's central telephone. By the time he had managed to say F-F-F-F-Findhorn, callers were in danger of thinking they had dialled the wrong number. Bella was not wanted in the kitchen, where she might have invented some vegetarian dishes more edible than those that regularly drove me into town in search of a not-so-spiritual hamburger. Instead, she was assigned first to the dining room, where she learned to "set the tables with love"; then later to the barnyard, where she tended and gathered eggs from more than a hundred chickens. My duties were in the Housekeeping Department, servicing the guest rooms and spot-cleaning endless metres of carpet with a toothbrush. Then later in the community's now well-composted and not-so-magical garden, where some were still in touch with the nature spirits, but where I scarcely knew the difference between a dandelion and a daffodil.

Most of the community's 300 members were seriously into what today would be called *woo*. Not always conducive to making rational decisions—which, as custom dictated, had to be reached by a consensus of all the members in attendance at community meetings in the Universal Hall. The result was, in my not-so-humble opinion as a clever organizational consultant, nothing less than chaos and potential economic disaster.

But two months into our probationary period, no one wanted to know what Dr. Dickinson thought needed to be done. With more than a hint of panic, I was wondering if we had made a dreadful mistake in coming here. I had just turned forty-five. The years were ticking by. Surely, with all my education, I could be doing something more useful with my life than spot-cleaning carpet in the Cluny Hill Hotel. Perhaps I wasn't ready for a Spirit-led community. We could return to Greensboro. The consulting firm would be glad to have me back, as would members of our family. Our as-yet-unsold house was there waiting for us. Nor would a juicy sirloin steak at The Pepper Mill, just off Guilford College Road, go amiss.

Such were the concerns, the anxieties, the increasingly urgent questions about my life direction that were brewing in me, never far from the forefront of my mind, as on that snowy New Year's Eve we turned the page on another decade.

I don't know exactly what time it was—I think around 3:00 or 4:00 in the morning—when I awakened in the dark of our room to find myself in a most unusual state of consciousness. A truly remarkable state of consciousness that I had never experienced before. I couldn't make out whether I was seeing/understanding something with astonishing clarity, or whether something was being revealed to me. It didn't matter. Either way it was the same. Translating the understanding/revelation into words, it went something like this:

> *Your being here at Findhorn is perfect. What is being burned out of you* (as if in reference to the mild flu-like fever I had been running a couple of days earlier) *is your need to believe that there is something you should be doing. I/we tell you* (the first-person singular and plural were blurred into one) *there is nothing you can do to make any significant difference. This form-level world is nothing*

but shifting sand dunes, and in the chaos that is to come everything will be changed. (The nature of the chaos was unclear, but it felt vaguely like catastrophic war in some troubled corner of the world.) *The only thing you need do is make inner connections.*

Only in retrospect can I say that none of this made any sense to me. Nor had I any idea what it meant to "make inner connections." At the time, I wasn't *thinking* anything. Then I heard a knocking at our bedroom door. Three sharp knocks in rapid succession that communicated an *imperative* beyond description. I knew that this was happening "within me" rather than "out there." But it was *as if* I heard an audible knocking at the door, and I was terrified. I knew I had the choice to say "Come in" or not, but the imperative was such that there was no real option. Feeling very small and sobbing now, I said "Come in." And into the room came a *Presence* that filled every nook and cranny of the space.

I had never before taken seriously any notion of divine judgment. But I immediately recognized this Presence as that of *Absolute Judgment*. It held not the slightest hint of anger or criticism. Only a quality/power so infinitely beyond me that my whole life was instantly laid out before me in all its petty triviality. I was simply and utterly judged *in the light of this Presence*. A verse from St. John's Gospel came to mind—"This is the judgment, that the light has come"°—as I tried to reassure myself with the thought that, if this is a Higher Presence, it must be a loving Presence. Instantly, as if telepathically, I received this response:

> *Yes, I/we are a loving Presence. And it is unlike anything you have ever thought of as love. It is a love that is infinitely demanding, and what is demanded is total transformation.*

This was not the least bit reassuring to me. But the Presence continued:

> *For some time you have been asking/praying that I/we come into your life and guide you so that your destiny may be fulfilled. You should know that this is happening. But*

> *you do not know what you ask. It is not something easy. It requires total transformation. It requires a purification and a burning away of all ego-attachments.*

This carried with it the feeling of "You asked for it; you got it." Then, in my terror, I wondered if I was dying. And, again, the thought received an instant, telepathic response:

> *No, you are not dying, though it's true that death is something like this. Be assured that you will live to fulfil your destiny. You are already past the point of no return and couldn't go back even if you wanted to. Your being here at Findhorn is a preparation. Do what you like while you are here; structure your time however you like, because it doesn't matter and should not be taken seriously. Only do the work of making inner connections. And know that your destiny is being fulfilled.*

By now I was flooded with tears of gratitude. I had no doubt as to the "reality" of what I had experienced. It was self-authenticating. And I was left feeling enormously blessed, humbled and grateful that I had been *visited* in this way. Visited by what or by whom, who could say? This *Presence* was beyond words. Beyond all comprehension. Rather than try to package it in some tidy mental construct, I was content to let it be a *mystery*. Whatever it was (and *this* was the gift, the blessing), I knew it could be trusted. I didn't know how to proceed or how to make inner connections. But *I was in process. Past the point of no return.* Despite my addiction to *doing*, despite all my foolish efforts to manage and manipulate my world, I knew now that the process can be trusted. I am in the hands of something infinitely greater than myself. And *my destiny is being fulfilled.*

~

During the next three days, it was as if there was no one at home. I was going through all the motions—engaging in my work, speaking with friends, and so on—but *I wasn't really there*. And I have a clear memory, almost a physical sensation, of returning. It was very much like an old Hertz Rent A Car television commercial, in which a man descends from the sky and lands behind the steering wheel of a convertible, to the accompanying words "Let Hertz put you in the driver's seat."° That's how it felt. Almost with a jolt, I *landed* back in my body. Later, Eileen Caddy told me that she and others had been concerned about me and had been praying for my safe return.

Some six months later, I attended a weeklong course that delivered impossible-to-understand lectures on *esoteric philosophy*. I remember thinking at the time that this was about as crazy as being in George Orwell's *Animal Farm*.° But then our mentor described a series of seven spiritual *initiations* through which people are said to pass over the course of many lifetimes—the third of which, he said, is called *the knock at the door*. He then described precisely what I had experienced in the early morning hours of that New Year's Day. I was stunned. He explained further that this initiation involves being taken out of one's body for three days to be imprinted with some otherwise inaccessible wisdom. Stunned again! Despite my skepticism, I would love to believe that such things are true. But considering my often-embarrassing lack of wisdom over the ensuing years, I have no evidence whatsoever to suggest that any such imprinting ever took place.

Then, still later in our year as members of this strangely wonderful community, as Bella and I were walking one day near the Community Centre, Eileen Caddy and another woman we didn't know approached us. Eileen introduced us to her companion. She was a world-renowned psychic who was visiting our community. We had scarcely exchanged greetings when she looked intently at me and said, with a note of surprise in her voice, something like "My God! Your heart chakra is opening more and more! It's wonderful! You have been through an initiation." Now I don't pretend to know about the chakras, but I immediately knew that what this woman said was true. Something was happening in me. Something was opening in me. I was in process. And our being here at Findhorn was instrumental in this process. Could it be that, despite myself, and without knowing what it meant, I was making inner connections? Which are actually *heart connections*?

∾

In the immediate aftermath of my New Year's Eve visitation from on high, still during that first week of January, as I was walking by myself one afternoon in the wooded glade behind Cluny Hill Hotel, I chanced again upon the tiny cemetery we had first discovered during our Experience Week. And I remembered having thought on that occasion, "I wonder if I'll be buried here." Now, in an instant, again as a kind of telepathic response to the thought itself, I was flooded with a vision. I know how crazy that sounds. But that was my experience. With my eyes wide open, I saw the sun setting over the South Pacific in what felt like New Zealand. It was the end of my life. The world had suffered some enormous upheaval, and now had a feeling of springtime freshness. Together humanity had learned, through all the chaos, that we have no option but to love one another.

The rest of our year at Findhorn was occupied with doing what had to be done to emigrate to New Zealand. Residency there could be granted only to those between the ages of eighteen and forty-five, and both Bella and I had just turned forty-five. There was no time to waste. Beyond that, one of us needed to be guaranteed a job in a work category that the country needed. These eminently sane antipodean islands, I was told, did not need another psychologist, but I'd be welcome as a Minister of Religion. So, in due course, despite my disregard over many years for anything remotely churchy, the Methodist Church of Aotearoa (that's the Maori name for New Zealand: it means "land of the long white cloud") agreed to gamble on me and appointed me as minister of a Co-operating Methodist–Anglican parish in the farming community of Okato, at the base of 9000-foot-high Mount Taranaki. Effective from February 1, 1981.

The one remaining obstacle to the realization of our now-shared vision was financial. After all those months, our house in Greensboro still hadn't sold. Our tenants were insisting that it needed to be repainted. And we were rapidly running out of money. It would be impossible, we decided, to follow through on our plans to emigrate unless the house was sold by October 31 — a week before the annual conference of the Methodist Church, when parish appointments for the ensuing year would be confirmed. If we had to bail out, we reckoned, the Church would still have time to make other arrangements.

Three days before that deadline, though scarcely able to afford the trip, we travelled by train to London for a face-to-face visa interview at the New

Zealand embassy. All went well. We were granted our visas. And with only thirty-six hours to go before calling New Zealand to say that our plans had to be abandoned, we received and accepted an offer on our Greensboro house.

If ever I had reason to believe in miracles, this was it. Tears of joy and gratitude streamed down my face as, not knowing what to do with myself, I walked alone in a drenching rain, through nighttime darkness, over Hampstead Heath. This was something to make even the angels laugh. I could almost hear them. Almost see the lights of home all around me. Heaven had never seemed so near.

⁓

The next three years of serving as a parish minister in Okato were enough not only to justify our New Zealand residency but also to make clear again what I had known many years before—that this was not my thing. Some in the congregation were less than happy at my speaking kindly of the Buddha, and even less so at the invasion of barefoot hippies who lived in a nearby mountain commune. Attracted by our Findhorn connection and my particular understanding of the gospel, they would, to the consternation of the faithful, sometimes appear at Sunday worship and provide guitar accompaniment to our typically lacklustre hymns of praise.

True to form, Bella insisted on enjoying herself. One day, just before we left the parish, she was invited for afternoon tea to the home of a parishioner who, to use a Yiddish term that Bella liked, was regarded as a *gantseh macher*—literally a "doer of everything," or more colloquially a "big cheese." As Beryl was preparing the tea, she said, "You know, Bella, you have been a great disappointment to us as a vicar's wife." To which Bella, unable to believe that anyone could fail to like her, replied, "Well, you haven't been so shit-hot yourself, Beryl." So much for afternoon tea. In gales of laughter, Beryl broke open a bottle of sherry, and they proceeded to enjoy together an altogether hilarious afternoon.

For the next five years, Bella and I lived co-operatively with others in the North Island city of New Plymouth, where as a group we created Dayspring: A Centre for the Development of the Whole Person. I was beginning to get the hang of making *inner connections* and, for the first time in my life, felt that I was in synch with my destiny. We provided a pay-what-you-can psychotherapy service that was available to everyone, and hosted seminars and workshops led by whatever spiritual luminaries happened to be visiting New Zealand. Including on one occasion a Tibetan Buddhist who was said to be a genuine bodhisattva and who was so extraordinarily ordinary that I was left wondering, "If the Messiah were to come smoking Cuban cigars and enjoying Scotch whisky, could he or she possibly be the Messiah?"

In 1989, attracted by the possibility of expanding our Dayspring venture in a larger city, Bella and I moved to Christchurch, on New Zealand's beautiful South Island. It has been my home ever since. Prompting me now to end this chapter of our lives by singing briefly the praises of this wonderful little country of fewer than five million people and nearly thirty million sheep. Apart from its scenic grandeur, it may just be the most democratic country in the world. Where ordinary citizens are *mates* (to use a time-honoured Kiwi word) with their highest-ranking government representatives. Where we were astonished to learn, soon after our arrival, that Prime Minister David Lange often picked up hitch-hikers on his way to work in the morning. Where Prime Minister Jenny Shipley once dropped by for lunch at a restaurant Bella managed. So delighted was she by Bella's homemade muffins that together they christened them "Jenny's muffins" and made a sign to that effect. Or where I sat one afternoon in Prime Minister Mike Moore's living room, discussing with him some business proposal, while his Polynesian wife served us tea. Or where, one evening, when a small group of us were dining *alfresco* in a boutique hotel, Prime Minister John Key came by, asked if he could join us, and spent the next ninety minutes in earnest conversation with us about the state of the nation.

How blessed we have been to spend these years *down under!* Who knows whence came that vision in the tiny cemetery behind Cluny Hill Hotel? Or why my destiny lies here? Or why the task of making *inner connections,* revealed to me on that winter's night at Findhorn, should finally be accomplished for me now in this gracious breaking open of my heart? But I thank whatever gods may be that this is so.

∿ ELEVEN ∿
SECOND DEATH

Now here I am, all these years later. Still in process. Learning to trust the process. Wanting to surrender to the process.

You are' past the' point of no return.
Your destiny is being fulfilled.

I've come to think that's all there is. That *everything* is process. It's all shifting sand dunes. Myself included. Nothing is static. Our language supports the illusion that there are nouns—more or less static, separate, and identifiable *things*. But in reality it's all a verb. *I am a verb.* Forever in process. "Everything flows," said Heraclitus more than 2500 years ago. "No man ever steps in the same river twice."°

So too my experience of grief is ever-changing. We call it *the grief process* because we like to think we know what we're talking about. "Oh yes, that's the grief process," we say knowingly. But it's not that simple. Not that tidy. My grief is mine. Just as yours is yours. And perhaps for you *and* me, it's part of a so-much-larger process called *fulfilling our destiny.* As we travel, homeward bound, on life's trajectory. Which in my case at least has something to do with making *inner connections*. Which in turn has very much to do with the breaking open of my heart on that Friday morning in spring when Bella and I and the cherry tree were, each in our own way, very much in process.

Some two months after Bella died, my grief took a distressing turn. The recurring and reassuring sense of Bella's presence became less frequent and began to fade. She was becoming less a living presence and more just a cherished memory. Tears were still easily triggered, but the grief was less intense. I was, as folk like to say, "getting on with my life." Struggling to accept my new reality: living out the rest of my days without my beloved. Bella was gone. *Dead and gone.* End of story. What option do I have but to let her go, pick up the pieces, and get on with it? Except that I don't *want* to get on with it. Or over it. Or through it. I want to continue grieving. It is the expression of my love. It feels rich and deep and wet and wonderful. Truly, *grief is just another word for love.* And I don't want either to end. Ever.

I later learned that this distressing turn is sometimes called *the second death.* I had been corresponding with Mitch Hodge—a cognitive scientist at Queen's University Belfast—about a paper he had coauthored: a report on recent research that identified certain "universal cognitive aspects of afterlife beliefs." The paper contained some comments that resonated deeply with my own experience.

> I don't believe in an afterlife, but I certainly "hope" that all the loved ones I have lost still survive and that I will see them someday. No matter how hard I dwell on my disbelief, it still takes a great deal of effort to imagine those I have loved as annihilated.
>
> The distinction that must not be lost is between intuitive, implicit beliefs and reflective, explicit beliefs. The secular conception of death as annihilation of the individual is a reflective, explicit belief, while the evidence shows that afterlife beliefs are intuitive and implicit. Our reflective, explicit beliefs interfere and override (with cognitive effort) our intuitive, implicit beliefs all the time.
>
> At a reflective, deliberative level, people "hope" there is an afterlife. But all the research points to an intuitive, implicit belief that we do, indeed, survive death. … For those of us who do hold the secular conception of death, whether we have been taught or reasoned into it, it is the intuitive pull of afterlife beliefs that keeps the hope alive in us.°

Exploring more of what Mitch and his colleagues had written, I came across another of his papers: "The Death We Fear Is Not Our Own." It exactly described my own experience. According to Hodge, cross-cultural research shows that we are afraid not so much of our own death or non-existence as of that of those we love. Especially those we have loved most deeply. The virtually universal grief experience delivers a sense of the loved one's presence, as if he or she is in another place, watching over us. This sense of presence, he claims, is an intuitive human response to the loss and a way of mitigating the almost unbearable pain of that loss.°

What made me wince, however, was the research evidence that accompanying this experience is the fear that we will lose this sense of presence—as indeed always eventually happens in what Hodge calls the *second death*. This was precisely what I had feared. That, like my memories, my grief would also fade. And that when my grief had run its course, I would no longer feel Bella's presence.

My distress, and my struggle to come to terms with this second death, are expressed in journal entries like the following.

This morning, as I walked to the coffee shop, I was reflecting on what Mitch Hodge had written about the *second death* and feeling immensely troubled by it. The only consolation I could find was in thinking, "I am glad that it's me and not Bella who is suffering this misery. By dying first, she has escaped the pain of this grief." I am not normally given to being a martyr, but my being the one to suffer this grief felt like the one last loving thing I could do for her.

And then, this afternoon, again while walking near my home, I suddenly and unexpectedly felt her presence again, as if she was prompting me to remember. So, on arriving home, I immediately "sat" and "listened" and received this message:

There need be no words; simply know that I am here.

Listen for every prompting, every reminder that I am always
    with you.
Your mind cannot possibly comprehend the reality of how it is,
and so it constantly doubts what your heart intuits to be true.
So listen for my prompting and trust your heart's response.
I feel such love, such compassion for you.

That seemed like the end—but after a couple of minutes, the message continued:

You cannot be with me always,
because you must attend to all that your life requires.
As you are able more and more to return to the everyday
    requirements of living,
it will sometimes seem that you are losing touch with me.
But I will never leave you; I am always here.
All you need do is remember that, and I will be present
    to you.

This seemed to suggest not so much that Bella is withdrawing from me as that I am withdrawing from her. Of necessity. As I become more engaged in life again. This, she seemed to be saying, is as it must be. But I can always return (and she may sometimes prompt me to do so) and be with her again.

———————————

I am very much afraid that I may be getting over my grief and "getting on with my life." Will Bella become no more than a memory? Is she already no more than a memory? Could my recurring, but now fading, sense of Bella's presence have been nothing but a concoction of my grief-stricken mind?

    I want so much to believe that this life so full of joy and suffering does not run out into nothing. So I struggle to maintain and pray for faith—which, for me, means holding fast to what my heart intuits to be true. The grey emptiness of my life, however, is fraught with this nagging fear of what Mitch Hodge has called the second death.

During last night's meditation, and again in my wanting to connect with Bella this morning, there was no sense of inner connection. I felt dry. It was hard to still my mind. And any sense of Bella felt like I was conjuring her up in my memory and imagination. But then, as I was getting dressed, I touched her clothes still hanging in the wardrobe and was immediately overcome with tears of grief. *And it felt so good.* As if a dam had burst. So good to know that my grief is still there, waiting only for the slightest touch to trigger and release it.

So I sat, as is my custom now, to be with Bella. At first there were no words. Just a tearful and deeply loving *communion* with her. As if we were silently together *in love*. I felt her pure and steady love for me, of which her actual love for me in this life was a wonderful approximation (so much steadier and more faithful than mine), while I tearfully expressed my love and gratitude for her. And then these words came to mind.

I am always here, my love;
nothing changes that.
Even if you no longer sense my presence
and I seem, as you fear, no more than a memory,
I am always here.
In a realm where there is no space or time,
there is no place else to be.
So do not be afraid, my love;
reality is perfect, and all is well.

My loneliness last evening was even greater than usual. It's as if the reality of Bella's departure is finally hitting home. The house, my days, my life feel painfully empty without her. And when I awoke this morning, my life was again a colourless grey. I could put in my time—walk to the coffee shop, do some writing, plan what I'd have for dinner, and buy groceries—but there was nothing I could look forward to. My heart was in none of it. Without Bella to share it, my life seemed reduced to mere existence. So when I sat to connect with her, I found myself saying "Sweet darling, you know how much I love you and am missing you." And this was the response:

I know.
It's difficult, my love.
I want so much to help –
to reassure you that it's all okay.
Your life will never be the same again –
the hopes and dreams, the fun and laughter that we shared,
    are gone.
Even though I am with you always, all that has been lost,
and the loss leaves your life feeling dull and grey.
All this is as it must be, at least for now.
But don't lose heart, my love; everything changes; your life is
    different now.
Go with the changes, darling. Trust the process. Feel the grey.
Your loss is real, but our love remains and I am always
    with you,
wanting so much to help and comfort you.

Last night I pictured my life as a circle composed of many components, all held together by their connection with the centre. At the centre was my relationship with Bella. Our love, our partnership. It's what gave meaning to my life.

Now, with that centre missing, all the other components, which were meaningful *because* they were linked to Bella and me, feel like free-floating and meaningless fragments. Nor can I imagine what else might come to constitute that unifying centre in my life.

Although I wasn't aware of contemplating this when I first "sat" this morning, this is what came to me almost immediately.

Your brokenness will heal,
and you will feel whole again.
It's just a temporary reorganization of your life.
I will always be at, or near, the centre of your life,
but now in a spiritual rather than a physical way.
This inner spiritual connection will become ever more
*   important and more real to you.*

This outer world is but a reflection —
an ever-changing reflection of an inner reality.
Life is a school in which, painfully, we learn to love.
That love, which is greater than simply "our love,"
can now be at the centre of your life.
Your lesson now is to be that love,
and express that love in every situation and circumstance of
*   your life.*

I feel myself swinging between depression—not wanting to get up and face the day—and a growing acceptance of my new reality. "Death is part of life," I tell myself. "A zillion people have lost their partner. That's what happens. That's how it is. So stop feeling sorry for yourself."

Then, this afternoon, I watched for the first time the DVD recording of Bella's Memorial Service. I hadn't felt able to watch it until now. It brought back tears, but not the kind of anguish I had feared. In fact, with a more objective eye, I was appreciating how well the DVD had been put together. Later, I phoned Johnny, who had filmed the DVD, and thanked him for doing such a great job. He remembered the service well, which "as a Christian," he said, he very much appreciated. I liked that.

Still later, in the evening, I sat quietly for a while in a small nearby park. Watching the trees rustling in the breeze and listening to a birdsong, I thought "All this, like Bella's life, is a wondrous manifestation of an unfathomable Mystery from which we arise, to which we return, and from which we are never separate." It was the same theme that had been running throughout the day. No longer present in the same way, Bella is one with the Eternal, and I am getting on with my life.

———————————

My sense of Bella's presence is definitely changing—from a sense of her being immediately present, to a sense that she has been absorbed into the Eternal. Or into God, if one prefers theistic language. She still feels accessible, but not in the way I had previously experienced. Her presence now has scarcely a trace of personality. It seems rather like a spiritual presence of pure love and care for me.

I wonder, could this same pattern of experience— the unexpected sense of the departed person's presence, followed a few weeks later by what Mitch Hodge calls the second death—account for the strange New Testament reports of Jesus' resurrection and ascension? Certainly he had been greatly loved by his closest followers, to whom his untimely death was almost beyond comprehension. Assuming that he had not, by some miracle, been physically resuscitated on that first Easter morning, one can understand how the disciples' sense of his afterlife presence was of enormous importance to them. But he was present to them only "during forty days," after which, according to the account of his ascension, "he parted from them" and "a cloud took him out of their sight."° Could it be that it is precisely this pattern of *afterlife presence* followed by a *second death* that has been mythologized at the heart of the Christian tradition?

While I hunger for the nearer sense of Bella's presence, I suspect that what is happening is as it must be. As my wounded heart heals and I gather my scattered self together and actively engage in life again. So when I sat to be with Bella this morning, there were no words. It was enough, and seemed appropriate, that I simply *be* in her now-ascended presence, or however we think of that Transcendence or Eternal Presence to which we all belong.

This afternoon, I went again to the park, to where her ashes are scattered. As I remembered walking with her there, I missed her hugely, and there were tears of great love. But these were only memories of the way we were. Now it's as if she has ascended. Still present, but ascended. And I am learning to live without her.

On awakening this morning, it seemed that Bella had gone. As I sat and tried to inwardly listen, the heavens were silent and empty. Then later, while walking home from the coffee shop, a wave of grief swept through me. I desperately wanted Bella to be with me. Her death has left such an enormous hole in my life. I can hardly deal with the emptiness. To accept that she has simply *gone* remains virtually impossible.

It seemed to me that Bella is where I *belonged. We belonged together.* I belonged with her as I have belonged nowhere else. Yes, I belong with my sons—but they are geographically far removed, and we are able to spend little time together. Besides, my belonging with them is a very different kind of belonging than that which existed (I hate writing that word in the past tense) with Bella. In a real sense, she was my *home*. And now I feel homeless. Unable to imagine any place or anyone that could ever feel like home to me again.

Except for this new and emerging possibility that I have fleetingly glimpsed! Could it be that, in this emptiness, I may come to know a deeper Presence? A kind of spiritual home to which we all belong and which even now holds Bella in its embrace? My love for her seems to open onto a still deeper and more inclusive love. It seems to be leading me to a still more profound belonging to that which is eternal.

At first I thought, "How can I live without you?" Now, as the days go by and I am in fact living without my beloved, there's a growing acceptance that I can do this. My life requires it.

Whether I'm intuiting how it really is or simply creating a belief that enables me to live without her, who can say? But I am choosing to believe that Bella has been taken up into the Divine, into the Transcendent One, into the Eternal Presence from which we can never be separate. And that she lives on now in this Ocean of Love that some of us call God. And, like a lens, focuses that Love in her own distinctive way.

Last night, in what seemed a timely serendipity, I watched a movie called *The Portrait of a Lady*—directed by New Zealand's own Jane Campion, and based on the Henry James novel of the same name. At the end of the film, when Ralph (played by Martin Donovan) is dying of consumption, he confesses to his cousin Isabel (played by Nicole Kidman) his lifelong secret love for her. "The pain is passing," he says, "but the love remains. Keep me in your heart, and we shall be closer than we have ever been."°

That is precisely how it seems to me.

~

I am learning, learning, learning to trust this ever-changing process. Learning to trust that, despite my resistance, despite my reluctance to "get on with my life," life moves me on in any case. Seemingly (and often to my astonishment) on what feels like this homeward-bound trajectory. Discovering en route that hidden in what I most fear are unexpected gifts.

I know how Pollyanna-ish this sounds. I could as well be spouting clichés like "even the darkest cloud has a silver lining." Though I suspect that even our most well-worn clichés contain truths that we too easily dismiss just because they have become clichés. So I hasten to add that what I am recounting here is *my* experience. Which may be very far from *your* experience. Especially if you're a refugee who has just lost your entire family in Aleppo or Mosul. Or if you are risking your life in a rubber dinghy on the Mediterranean, fleeing the misery and war-torn strife of North Africa in hopes of a better life in Europe. My life, by contrast, has been a cakewalk. So forgive me if I dare to share with you what has been, for me, this most wondrous gift of a broken heart. Or if I spout what sounds to you like just another cliché about "trusting the process."

Such trust is what I've come to understand as *faith*—though that's not an entirely new idea to me. Before Bella and I moved to Greensboro, when I was still casting about for job opportunities in the U.S. Sun Belt, I had sent my resumé to James N. Farr & Associates—the consulting firm with which I would later be employed. Having received no reply to my application, I phoned the company one morning and spoke directly with Jim Farr. He had just returned from vacation, he said, and had not had a chance to review the many applications he had received. But, since I was on the phone, he agreed to look at my application then and there. After a few minutes of perusing it, he said, in what was his characteristically less-than-gentle mode of speech, "It says here that you're a goddam preacher. Tell me, what the hell is faith?" To which, in a moment of inspiration, I replied, "Faith is the opposite of belief." To which he in turn replied, "Well, I'll be damned. You'd better get your ass on down here." And so began that chapter of our life.

Though I scarcely knew what I was saying at that time, I have since come to understand that faith indeed has nothing to do with belief—at least not in the sense of "belief in some religious doctrine or article of faith." It is trust. Trust in what your heart intuits to be true and in where your intuition wants to lead you. In the Bible, it is epitomized by Abraham. Called by God to leave his home country and "go out to a place he was to receive as an inheritance, he went out not knowing whither he went."° That may not be living sensibly or prophylactically. It may be dangerous. And almost certainly exciting. But more and more it seems to me the only way to go. Listen to your heart and trust the process. "You are past the point of no return. And your destiny is being fulfilled."

So this has been my process since the morning Bella died. When the pain and anguish of a broken heart delivered this blessed gift of knowing, at a so much deeper level than I had ever known before, that we are all inseparably one in an ocean of love. And then discovering that, beyond the dreadful fear of finally and forever losing Bella in a *second death*, her now-ascended presence is introducing me to depths of *inner connection* that feel like a culmination both of our love story and of my spiritual odyssey.

∼ TWELVE ∼
WHEN "DEEP CALLS TO DEEP"

During Bella's childhood in Wales, most of her friends and schoolmates were from Christian families who, on Sunday mornings, attended "chapel," as the Baptist church was called. Sometimes Bella went with them. She liked singing the hymns—especially "Onward, Christian Soldiers"° and "Courage, Brother, Do Not Stumble."° Those were the war years, and bombs were falling not far away on the Cardiff dockyards. Singing hymns like these and asking God to "please kill Adolf Hitler" were her contribution to the war effort. Though she said the war never frightened her. On the contrary, it was fun. The blackouts. Going with her mother to the air-raid shelter in the middle of the night, equipped with her very own gas mask in its Mickey Mouse container. And being confronted en route by a neighbour, a member of the Home Guard, who would always challenge them with "Who goes there? Friend or foe?" But Bella could make almost anything seem like fun. Not until the end of the war did she learn what had happened to Europe's Jews.

On one of these Sunday mornings in the chapel with her friends, she was invited to read the 23rd Psalm from the lectern—an event sufficiently unusual to be reported the next morning in the Merthyr Tydfil *Times* and prompting the Rabbi to call on Bella's mother to protest her daughter's less-than-kosher behaviour. To which her mother responded by rebuking the Rabbi for his prejudice and ordering him from the house. It was for Bella a memorable moment. A lesson in tolerance and interfaith respect that, in years to come, would serve her well as New Zealand's only Jewish vicar's wife.

Although, as a young girl, Bella enjoyed her family's annual celebrations of Hanukkah, the gifts exchanged on these occasions seemed paltry compared with the mountains of gifts she saw beneath the festooned Christmas trees of her Christian friends. She was envious. So when, many years later, we made our own home together, Christmas was celebrated lavishly, in contrast to the more perfunctory nod we gave to Hanukkah. And Bella was always immensely generous—and thoughtful—in the gifts she chose.

One Christmas morning, when we lived in Greensboro, I found beneath the tree a beautifully wrapped gift, within which I discovered another beautifully wrapped gift, within which in turn was yet another—all nested together like Russian dolls. Layer upon layer of ever more generous gifts. The first was a pair of socks. *Hello!* I thought: *How strange is this? Bella buying me socks?* But with the socks was another box, containing a necktie. And then another, containing an exquisite dress shirt by some Italian designer. The final box contained a card on which was written, with poetic endearments, instructions to look in the guest-bedroom wardrobe. The last layer had been reached. The most beautifully tailored suit that I would ever own. Made from the finest worsted wool. Although how Bella managed to pass on my measurements to the tailor without my knowledge has remained a mystery.

I think of this now because the gift of a broken heart is like that. It has been, to my surprise, multilayered. And is still in the process of being unwrapped. The gift revealed at each stage of this grief process opens onto a still more surprising and unexpected gift. First, a tsunami of love that is not so much *my* love as an *ocean* of love to which we all belong and in which there is no separation. Followed by the gift of Bella's continuing presence and the assurance that she remains closer even than my breathing. Followed in turn, beyond all my fears of a *second death*, by a blessed sense that she has been taken up into the heart of God and that eternity itself now bears the imprint of my beloved.

Nor is that the end of it. I don't know how to say this in any way that makes sense. But over the months that have ensued since Bella's death, my still very open and vulnerable heart has more and more opened into realms of inner experience that I dare to think are glimpses of enlightenment. Not that this should be surprising. If, as all our spiritual traditions maintain, there is within us a potential shift in consciousness variously called *satori* or *moksha* or *eternal life*, it would be surprising if we ordinary mortals never had at least a glimpse of that state. But what *is* surprising, and may come *only* as a surprise, is that whatever glimpse is given us seems always courtesy of an open heart. And more surprising still, to me at least, is that this should be the gift of a *broken* heart. The multilevel gift of a broken heart that is still in the process of being unwrapped.

The Christmas-gift analogy is apt in another way too. Just as the discovery of each new gift-within-a-gift moves in an inward direction, so I feel that I am being opened inward to ever-deeper levels of myself. Now, with the disclosure of this deepest-level gift, an inner connection seems to have been made between my own depths and the Sacred Depth of an Ultimate Reality to which we all belong. As if a surface wave on the ocean, which for so long has imagined itself to be a separate something, suddenly discovers in its own depths its connection to, its oneness with, the ocean as a whole. Could this be the *inner connection* to which I was pointed on that New Year's Eve at Findhorn? Could it be the same inner experience of which the Psalmist sang some 2500 years ago?

> Deep calls to deep at the thunder of thy cataracts;
> all thy waves and thy billows have gone over me.°

Would that I could be so poetic! In nearly every instance, this calling of deep to deep has for me occurred during meditation. As often as not, my efforts to focus my attention and still my mind meet with failure. Mental chatter repeatedly carries me away. But sometimes, with no effort whatsoever, as I turn toward that inner realm where Bella seems embraced by the Eternal, I am met by grace. As if Bella is leading the way. An almost tangible flow of energy connects my head and heart and belly, filling my core and expanding into what feels like a sea of energy or an ocean of love in which I am immersed. Here there are no thoughts. Just a vast sea in which "deep calls to deep." And always it feels like a gift.

∽

Sometimes, in these experiences of grace, when this inner connection is made, I feel myself *fall* into a vast inner spaciousness that is paradoxically both empty and full. Into a sea that is utterly silent—and yet, I can almost hear its roar. At other times, this same spaciousness, this inner silence, is filled with an all-embracing Presence beyond all words. Though no description ever adequately captures it, I repeatedly attempt just that in journal notes made immediately after these experiences. Here are extracts from a few such journal entries.

For several days, my meditations have been very ordinary. "Nothing to write home about," as we used to say. But last night, as I prepared for bed, I sensed Bella's presence and a prompting to meditate. So I did. Very quickly, as I expressed my love for her, I filled with tears and my heart opened. Exactly what that means, I don't know. We speak casually about an "open heart," and the phrase is an apt description of what I experience—as if there is an almost tangible *opening* in the region of the heart. But why this should be so, I have no idea.

On this occasion, an inner portal seemed to open, just beneath my mind, through which I *fell*, gently, into a vast inner spaciousness that was perfectly still. With almost every breath, on the exhale, shivers of energy ran up and down my spine as if some energy connection had been made. They felt like *showers of blessing* delivering a kind of spiritual nourishment for which I was immensely grateful. My mind was silent as I rested in this peaceful, loving, timeless space where I felt totally connected, blessed, and inwardly nourished. It seemed that Bella had opened an inner door for me and made this possible. The entire experience, though extraordinary, was unspectacular. No bells and whistles! No heavenly choirs! Just this vast inner spaciousness and silence!

I easily remained in this space for at least thirty minutes, after which it seemed right to return to my usual state of mind and go to bed. It felt like returning to the surface—from the depths to this quite different level of myself where everyday life plays out. As I did, the word

Hridaya came to mind. An ancient term from the Hindu Upanishads, it means both "heart cave" and "spiritual portal." The Hindu sage Ramana Maharshi described it as "the dynamic Spiritual Heart." Through meditation, he said, "you can learn to find the Self in the cave of this Heart."° It seemed clear to me that this is where I had been. By whatever gift of grace, I had been given entrée, through this spiritual portal, to my heart cave.

Again, in last night's meditation, quickly and easily, I found myself in an inner place of vast unbounded spaciousness. There was no dissolving of my boundaries, as sometimes happens. Nor was it particularly blissful. I simply rested in a silent inner spaciousness. I was aware of myself as a locus of consciousness, of my breathing, and of the occasional itch. But it was difficult to think of anything. It required effort not to *stop* thinking but to have any thoughts at all. My mind just naturally remained quiet and undisturbed. It seemed that some powerful attraction had drawn me into this inner space from which it was difficult to escape. Or in which it was at least extremely tempting to remain.

The experience bore the slightly anxious hint that I might be dying. Or that dying may be like this. Or that it would be very easy to die if I let myself remain in this inner space. I both *wanted* to remain, because it felt like "home," *and* felt an urge to return to my usual and familiar world. To visit and be nourished here felt like a gift, and I was hugely grateful. But it wasn't right that I should stay. At least not yet. So, after about an hour, I roused myself and returned to bed. But even as I did, the sense of spaciousness remained. It was ever-present, just in the background. As if my ordinary life was taking place *within* this spaciousness. As if I have a dual nature. I am an individual locus of everyday consciousness in a sometimes itchy body. *And I am this spaciousness.*

How can I describe this? I *knew* that, in my individuality, I am so insignificant as to be virtually nothing. Nothing but a tiny ripple, less even than a wave, on this infinite sea. This little life, this sense of being "somebody," is nothing but the tiniest, fleeting flicker of consciousness. *And I am immense. I am this sea of consciousness. I am this unbounded spaciousness.* Both are true. I am the nothingness, and I am the everything. But why this should be so—why the infinitely creative rippling of the Boundless Sea should manifest as Merv or Bella or anything at all—remains a mystery.

This practice of meditation is a strange business. Quite unpredictable. With no guaranteed payoff. I can understand why so many people give up on it. For me, it has become a kind of punctuation point in the daily rhythm of my life. I think of it as doing my spiritual homework. A discipline that may prepare the ground for those fleeting *moments of connection* with which I am sometimes blessed. Often my mind remains too much in play, and I cannot find access to that inner place. At other times, for no apparent reason, what feels like *grace* (I don't know what else to call it) from what seems like a vertical eternal dimension (I don't know how else to describe it) enters the horizontal time-line of my life.

My meditation last night was like that. Almost as soon as I sat down, there was a strong sense of this other dimension—this inner space where deep calls to deep. I did not, as often happens, drop into it. Rather, it welled up within me from the depths, pervading my consciousness with an indescribable *fullness* that was at the same time *emptiness*. And a *silence* that at the same time had the *roar* of the ocean.

There were no thoughts. Or if an occasional thought did come to mind, it did not intrude on the silence, but effortlessly passed through. It was as if *contemplation* had taken the place of thinking. I'm not even sure what contemplation is. But it felt like the calm remembrance of a long-forgotten Truth, beyond all thought or words. A remembrance of the One to which, or to whom, we all belong.

What filled my consciousness seemed the eternal background out of which all else in my life emerges. In the background is this Ocean of Love, the Eternal One, this vast spacious emptiness/fullness that now and forever bears the imprint of Bella. In the foreground is this time-and-space dimension of my life. Both were present simultaneously. The whole experience felt like a gift. An unexpected blessing.

When eventually I returned to bed, the sense of this eternal background remained. And, to my surprise, was still present this morning. Throughout my walk to and from the coffee shop, I had the same blissful sense that everything— the trees, the traffic, everything, including my own brief sojourn here—was a wondrous manifestation of the One. It was as if I was seeing with my heart as well as with my eyes. It was extremely subtle, but enduring. And I wondered if it might be possible to live like this—in the midst of this multiplicity, in this astonishing world of "ten thousand things,"° with the inner knowing that it is all a wondrous manifestation of the One. Truly with a foot in both realms.

During last night's meditation I again seemed to drop through an inner portal into a vast, silent spaciousness. Had I inadvertently found the key? But on this occasion, I found myself inseparably one with what I can only describe as *Presence*—so all-encompassing that I want to spell it with a capital *P*. Not *a* Presence, or a sense of *me* being present. In fact, there wasn't any *me*. Just *Presence*, which pervaded and included everything. And a blissful sense of being "home."

There was no need to turn off my thinking mind. It simply stopped. But my individuality remained intact. I could even reflect, albeit gently, on what I was experiencing, without disrupting or leaving this inner space in which there was no separation. No sense of distance, however small, between "me" and what I was experiencing. It's as if I was floating in an inner space pervaded by Presence. A space that was totally calm and loving and connected. "Truth shivers" were almost continuously rushing up and down my spine. And tears began to flow—tears of gratitude, love, recognition. I cannot remember ever before feeling so open or so blessed.

When, after perhaps an hour, I returned to bed, this sense of Presence remained in the background as I drifted off to sleep. And when I woke this morning, to my surprise, I found myself still in this same calm and loving space. All my usual activities seemed to be occurring *within* this space. Everything I did was imbued with a loving calm and a continuing sense of Presence. And it continued throughout the day. As I went about my volunteer work at the hospice, the same lingering Presence seemed to hold us all—the patients, the nurses, and me—in its embrace.

As I write this now, the sense of Presence has faded but not gone. It remains in the background of my awareness. Everything is occurring *within* this Presence. I am an individual point of consciousness *within* this Presence. *And there is no separation.* The Presence is so all-pervasive, the Oneness so all-inclusive, that it seems *this is who I am.* Without losing any of my individuality, *this is who I am.* A wave on the ocean looks like an identifiable something, but it's just the ocean waving. So I am an expression of Eternal Presence. *Eternal Presence is Merving.*

It's impossible to express this in more rational terms. A Zen koan asks: "What is your original face before your

parents were born?" To which Dōgen Zenji, a 13th-century
Japanese Buddhist poet, replied:

> Cease from practice based
> On intellectual understanding,
> Pursuing words and
> Following after speech.
> Learn the backward
> Step that turns
> Your light inward
> To illuminate within.
> Body and mind of themselves
> Will drop away
> And your original face will be manifest.°

YES! That is exactly as it seems to be.

Having slept through the night last night, I did not meditate
until early this morning. And although I didn't, as on
previous occasions, fall into some inner spaciousness, I
did experience again a powerful sense of *Presence*. It was
not unlike my occasional sense of Bella's presence, except
that it was limitless. Nor was it separate from me. It was
not any*where*, but seemed rather like a timeless or eternal
dimension in which everything exists just as surely as we
exist in the dimensions of time and space.

The certainty of this brought tears to my eyes. Tears
of what, I don't know. Tears of joy/gratitude/recognition.
But as I wiped the tears away and opened my eyes, behold,
everything was pervaded by this Presence. It seemed to be
shimmering just behind the ordinary things in the room.
And I thought, "Wow! This is how it is! Everything is a
manifestation of this larger five-dimensional Reality. All that
we experience in time and space is but an expression of this

other dimension. Not of a supernatural world, but of another dimension of this incredible Reality that we are part of."

As I proceeded then to shower and get dressed and have my breakfast, and even as I drove through morning traffic into the city, this sense of *something else* just *behind* my ordinary experience continued. It seemed a gift for which I was hugely grateful.

It seems a long time since I've had any clear sense of Bella's presence. And in the interests of "getting on with my life," I have avoided my practice of deep listening. Upon awakening this morning, however, I had, if not a sense of Bella's presence, an impulse to once more sit and listen for anything she might have to say. This is what took shape in my mind:

Good morning, darling.
I know it's hard for you
to know, to fully comprehend,
all that is happening to you,
or that I am always with you.
The truth is, there is only Presence;
there is no place else to be.
Separation exists only in your mind.
As for death, it is only the body that dies.
Beyond the appearance of separation,
there is only Presence in which we are forever one.
So do not be dismayed, my darling.
The truth is more wonderful than anything you can
  imagine.

As I emerged from this place of deep listening, I thought: It will be enough—no, more than enough—if I can live the rest of my days against the backdrop of this eternal *Presence*.

Never doubting that all I have experienced and what Bella
has shared with me in these conversations is true.

I seem unable to resist trying to make sense of these experiences. I want to
know: is this how it *really* is? Or are these experiences, which are such a gift
to me, merely the result of some mental glitch? A delusion triggered by the
emotional intensity of grief? There is of course no way to answer that. Not
rationally or scientifically. It is a matter not for the head, but for the heart.
Still, I find it hard *not* to ask the question.

I recently shared some of these experiences, and my efforts to make
sense of them, with Kenneth Ring—arguably the world's leading expert on
near-death experiences. His reply startled me with its wisdom and simplicity.
He said, in effect, "You can of course spend your time struggling to explain
these experiences if that's what you need to do. But you'll never reach any firm
conclusion. So why not just accept your experience *without interpretation*—
without trying to assess whether it is true or not? Just let the experience
speak for itself." It was one of those "Aha!" moments. It hadn't occurred to me
that I didn't have to interpret or explain or make sense of everything—that
I didn't always have to assess the validity of my experience or make it fit some
rational worldview. Maybe I could just let it be what it is, in the same way
as I experience a Vivaldi concerto or the call of a bellbird on a clear spring
morning, and allow it to inform, or *trans*form, my life in whatever way it will.

Later, as I read again one of my most treasured books, Martin Buber's
I and Thou, the following words seemed to confirm what Ken Ring had said.
They weren't new to me, but now, in light of my own experience, they seemed
more exquisitely beautiful than ever:

> There are moments of silent depth in which you look
> on the world-order fully present. ... These moments are
> immortal, and most transitory of all; no content may be
> secured from them. ... The world which appears to you
> in this way ... comes even when it is not summoned,
> and vanishes even when it is tightly held. ... You cannot

make yourself understood with others concerning it,
you are alone with it. ... Through the graciousness of
its comings and the solemn sadness of its goings it leads
you away to the *Thou*. ... It does not help to sustain you
in life, it only helps you to glimpse eternity.°

I would like so very much simply to honour these moments of
connection. These transitory yet immortal moments when deep calls to deep.
These moments of silent depth beyond all understanding, which lead me
away to the *Thou* and enable me to glimpse eternity. And perhaps even re-
create my mundane life such that it can never be the same again.

∾ THIRTEEN ∾
LIVING AT THE INTERSECTION

It's now more than two years since Bella died, and the intensity of my grief is much diminished. As one would expect. Although I'm not sure why I say that: I'm new to this and have no basis for knowing what to expect. God knows, I would not have expected any of what I have experienced over these past months. But still, my grief is winding down. Not over, but winding down. It may in fact never be *over*, whatever that means. It's not like recovering from a prolonged illness, such that one can say "Whew! I'm glad *that's* over. I'm feeling fine again, thank you."

It's not like that at all—at least in my experience. I know there are those who, after a year or two, "move on," as people like to say. They partner up with someone else and seem quite happy doing so. Some among my own friends prod me gently in that direction. They say, "I think So-and-So is attracted to you. Why don't you invite her out for dinner?" I know they're concerned for me. They want the best for me. And I have no doubt that they too would feel better if they thought my grief was done and dusted. But I can't imagine this Bella-shaped space in my heart ever being filled by someone else. So not a day goes by that I'm not prompted by some memory to speak aloud to her: "Sweet darling. I love you so much. And miss you terribly."

But the *intensity* of my grief has clearly diminished. I am still sometimes surprised by tears, but less often. I no longer have that sudden, unexpected sense of Bella's presence. Nor does my heart any longer feel so open. Still tender and more easily opened than before. But no longer so *dramatically* open, so *broken* open, as in the days and weeks immediately following Bella's death. And truth be known, I don't ever want to lose this openness. A broken heart is an open heart. And if the natural course of grieving must inevitably bring closure to this blown-open heart, please God may I never lose the gifts it has delivered. Above all, this gift of *inner connection* to a realm that is eternal, beyond all time and space, where deep calls to deep and the love flows freely and I remember the vastness of who I am. Perhaps, if I am lucky, my heart will break over and over again to reveal new depths of love, allowing my heart each time to heal bigger than before. Expanding my capacity to love. And with every heartbreak, opening more and more into that ocean of love that is our spiritual home.

Whatever healing may be taking place, there are still occasions, thankfully, when something in the region of my heart opens into what feels like another dimension. My everyday world of space and time—this world of "ten thousand things"°—recedes into the background and gives way to a larger reality that, like another dimension, extends in a different direction. It's as if, inadvertently, I slip into a different mode of consciousness in which reality takes on this added dimension of which I'm usually unaware.

I think of this as a spiritual or mystical dimension. It does not, in my experience, point to any supernatural realm—unless by "supernatural" you mean that which cannot be explained by the laws of physics. Rather it seems like another dimension of *this* world, of this one reality that I ordinarily experience only in its time-and-space dimensions. And although I cannot, in scientific terms, account for it, or even find words to adequately describe it, there is an image I find helpful. It explains nothing, but goes some way toward describing what cannot be captured in words.

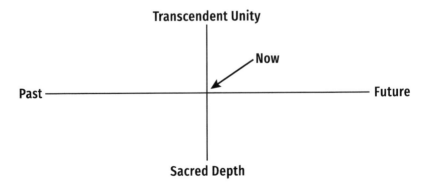

The horizontal line represents my ordinary, everyday experience in this four-dimensional world of space and time, delivered to me by my five senses and organized in a more or less coherent fashion by my mind. Here I experience myself as a separate being, occupying space along with countless others and moving along the time-line of however many years are mine to live. Here my experience is shaped by my mind—interpreting the sensory data, arranging to meet recurring needs, planning my future, and generally trying to keep the ship afloat as long as possible. And sometimes taking me to wherever absent-minded professors go when they ponder the mysteries of the universe and struggle to concoct a theory of everything.

The vertical line represents a quite different dimension, described by mystics and spiritual masters throughout history, but perhaps only rarely experienced by ordinary folk like me. Here there is no separation in space, and no time but the present. It intersects the time-line of my life in every now moment but is accessible only when I am present. That is, when my mind stops. When it takes a break from the busywork of doing what minds are meant to do. Or, as happened on the morning Bella died, when a present reality so overwhelms my mind, sweeping it away in a tsunami of love, that it is simply silenced. Rendered inoperative. Then my heart opens, and I enter through the narrow gate, through the portal of the ever-present now, into an infinitely spacious and eternal dimension where there is only Presence. Sometimes that feels, to me at least, like *Transcendent Unity*, and at other times like *Sacred Depth*. But this isn't a continuum: these are only different flavours of the same reality. Here my heart opens in both directions—into a transcendent, all-embracing One, and into an ocean of love where all the rivers meet, and deep calls to deep.

We live at the intersection of these two lines. *Now* is the only place that we can be. But I am usually *conscious* only of the horizontal plane. Not *present* to the transcendent One or to the depths of my own being. Only rarely do I gain access to the vertical dimension. Leaving me to wonder if it's even possible to be conscious simultaneously on both these planes—to live always in this expanded reality.

Martin Buber, the Hasidic mystic whose writings so inspire me, says no. The point of consciousness that each of us calls "I" stands in relation either to the space–time world of *It* or to the unnameable Presence that he calls *Thou*.

These are for him the "two poles of humanity."° We can swing between the two, but we can't be simultaneously at both. Or thinking of these as different dimensions, "the world of *It*," he says, "is set in the context of space and time. The world of *Thou* is not set in the context of either of these. Its context is in the Centre, where the extended lines of relations meet—in the eternal *Thou*."° He explains:

> It is not possible to live in the bare present. Life would be quite consumed if precautions were not taken to subdue the present speedily and thoroughly. But it is possible to live in the bare past, indeed only in it may a life be organized. ... And in all the seriousness of truth, hear this: without *It* man cannot live. But he who lives with *It* alone is not a man.°

If this be true, then please may my heart remain sufficiently open to be met, again and again, by grace and given entrée to this vertical dimension where I am inwardly nourished, and there is no separation, and love is all there is. Then when I return, as return I must, to this space–time world of *It*, may I never in my mind stray far from the intersection. Never forget what I have seen there to be true. And remember always the immensity of who I am. A tiny ripple on an ocean of love, whose *raison d'être* is to *be* that Love, here in this very ordinary life in this extraordinary world.

Opening to this vertical dimension is, I think, what must have been meant by the directive given to me on that New Year's Eve at Findhorn long ago: "The only thing you need do is make inner connections." Over all the years since then, I have struggled to understand what that means. But now it seems clear. Opening to this vertical dimension feels precisely like making an inner connection. Or rather *remembering* an inner connection that always exists. How can this tiny ripple *not* be connected to the vastness of the sea? It's who we are. But I so easily forget this in my everyday world, where everything appears so separate.

It seems clear too that this connection is remembered not with the mind, but with an open heart. And for some of us perhaps, only with a heart that has been broken open. Call it what you will—Self-remembering,°

making inner connections, or opening to this vertical dimension—this is, for me, the gift of a broken heart. And because it seems a culmination of the love story and the spiritual odyssey that we shared, I wonder if it's yet another gift sent with love from Bella.

∾

I can't help wondering too what difference, if any, all this makes in my down-here-on-the-ground everyday life. I mean, it's all well and good to spend time each night in meditation, and sometimes sink into a blissful state that feels like another dimension. But when morning comes and another day begins, do these blessed moments of connection make any difference? As the Zen proverb puts it: "After enlightenment, the laundry."° Exactly! When the laundry must be done and dinner prepared and the final chapter written, does living at the intersection, open to the vertical dimension, make any difference?

My own answer to that is "Yes and No." Depending on the kind of change you're looking for.

The No side is this. If you were to ask any of my friends, "Has Merv changed since Bella died?" I expect they would answer, "No. He's still the same old Merv"—though perhaps with more emphasis on "old" than would once have been the case. I can't be sure of that, since I haven't asked them. But that's my sense of it. To all outward appearances, I haven't changed. With the possible exception that I cry more readily. Tears are easily prompted now whenever I see or hear any expression of love. But this too can be explained as a lingering symptom of my grief. "He's still pretty vulnerable," my friends might say. "But he'll get over it eventually."

The Yes side is this. Although nothing outwardly has changed, on the inside everything has changed. *Everything has changed!* I may be the only one who knows this. But my life and my world are different now. I can feel it. And the change feels permanent. I can't imagine ever returning to the state of mind or consciousness I occupied before my heart was broken. I can't imagine ever *not* knowing what I have come to know at the intersection. That I, and we, and everything in this world of "ten thousand things"° are manifestations of an infinitely larger Reality in which there is no separation, even from those whom we have "loved … and lost awhile."°

No separation! That has been the recurring insight. And the key to all the associated changes I've experienced. *No separation!* How could it have taken me so long to know this? I've lived my entire life as if I'm separate. Loved and supported by family and friends, yes. But ultimately on my own. "We're born alone, we live alone, we die alone" was the sad conclusion reached by Orson Welles.° Here, on the horizontal plane, uninformed by any glimpses of eternity, our mind constructs a world where everything is separate in time and space. Where we manage our life and navigate this hazardous world as best we can.

Until, as if by grace, often in the midst of suffering, sometimes overwhelmed by grief, that world is one day swept away. Or rather, the barrier of perceived separation is swept away. By a tsunami of love. And we find ourselves standing, or kneeling, at the intersection with eternity. Here the mind stops: no more separation! The heart opens; there is only Presence. Here I *know* what, please God, I will never forget—that I am inseparably one with a Reality that is beyond, beyond, beyond. Beyond all thought, beyond all names, beyond all comprehension.

I'm sorely tempted to name this Reality. As if by naming it I'll be able to address it and relate to it and make it more accessible. The *Tao Te Ching* has been warning us against this for at least 2500 years: "The Tao that can be named is not the eternal Tao."° But still it's tempting. And because, at the intersection, our experience is one of *Presence,* and of *loving* Presence, it's so easy to personalize this Reality. *Thou* becomes an *It* named God, or Yahweh, or Allah, or Brahman, or Ahura Mazda, or whatever. These may be a useful shorthand for pointing to the Nameless One, but if we imagine they refer to a deity created in our own image, they are dangerous. Before we know it, we've created a belief system presumed to be the truth, in defence of which we may even go to war. Far better, as the mystics have always known, to remain silent before the Mystery. To heed the caution offered by Stephen Levine:

> Don't try to name it; you'll only start a holy war. That's why some call it the Unnameable. It is pure awareness before consciousness begins to stir. It is the space between thoughts. It is the ocean in which our tiny

bubble floats. It is the formlessness upon which form depends, the deathless which dies again and again just to prove it never dies.°

Still, I find myself searching for how I might speak, if only to myself, of what I still sometimes call God. The words that now most often come to mind are these:

> Beloved Mystery
> Transcendent Unity
> Unfathomable Depth
> Eternal Presence
> Ocean of Love
> Perfect Stillness
> This is Home

Could it be that all God's names are hallowed?

～

Once the barrier of separation has been dissolved or swept aside, other inner changes follow naturally. One is what Buber calls "the inexpressible confirmation of meaning."° In moments of inner connection, when the world of *It* becomes transparent to *Thou*, when fleetingly we glimpse the vertical dimension, "meaning," he says, "is assured":

> Nothing can any longer be meaningless. The question about the meaning of life is no longer there. ... You do not know how to exhibit and define the meaning of life, you have no formula or picture for it, and yet it has more certitude for you than the perceptions of your senses.°

That is precisely my experience. Not that I had previously thought of my life as meaningless. At least not in the way some existentialist writers have suggested. I rarely feel even mildly depressed, let alone burdened by

Kierkegaard's "despair"° or Camus' sense of "the Absurd."° But, like most people, I can't help wondering if there's any reason for my being here beyond ensuring the survival of my genes. What Viktor Frankl famously called "man's search for meaning" is deeply rooted in our human nature.° His 1946 book by that title had, by the time of his death fifty years after it was published, sold over ten million copies and been translated into twenty-four languages. Our search for meaning seems a universal and insatiable hunger. One that can't be met by any philosophical pronouncement. Or avoided by insisting that life is meaningless apart from the meaning we ascribe to it. Or alleviated by pursuing some purpose or another. Life is cluttered with purposes. But no purpose, even the most noble, ever satisfies the hunger.

Because meaning, it turns out, is not found in anything we do or achieve or believe, but in opening to an eternal dimension of Transcendent Unity and Sacred Depth. When, in moments of inner connection, we know, with more certitude than the perceptions of our senses, that we are inseparably one with an unnameable Reality that feels very much like home. Then the question of life's meaning no longer exists. The question arises only out of our felt separation on the horizontal plane. But here, at the intersection, meaning is assured. Our *experience* of it may be inexpressible. But its aftertaste can last a lifetime.

Another change taking place since Bella died is an expansion of my capacity for compassion. It's as if my broken heart has opened to a fuller flow of love and compassion. Again, I'm not sure whether this is recognizable in action. I think it should be. I mean, what good is love if it's not expressed? But if so, it's very subtle. All that I can say for sure is that I *feel* very different. This still very tender and vulnerable heart is more profoundly touched by the suffering of others, and responds with greater compassion.

Because this feels so new to me, often surprising me with its intensity, I've often tried to describe the experience in journal notes. Here are just a few.

Last night I watched a film titled *Brooklyn*.° It's a sweet, innocent love story, set in the 1950s, about a young Irish woman who emigrates to New York City, struggles with homesickness, falls in love and marries, returns to Ireland to visit her aging mother, and must come to terms again with where she truly belongs. In the end, she returns to New York City to be with her husband.

Repeatedly, throughout the movie, I found myself in tears. Not tears of sadness. There was nothing in the movie to be sad about. But tears of compassion. Tears of overflowing love for all of us who, like this young Irish woman, are struggling to be the best that we can be. It was as if an inner connection had been made, and Love from the Source was flowing through me.

On returning home, I was still feeling very open and vulnerable—an almost physical sensation in my heart—and close to tears. Which I found not just surprising but a little frightening. I don't know what's happening to me. It's as if, since Bella's death, I am being changed in some way. Rendered more open and vulnerable. All these feelings are so closely intertwined—grief, vulnerability, compassion, love. And I'm feeling them all acutely now.

In last night's meditation, I was anticipating the arrival tomorrow of my son Mark. It will be his first visit to New Zealand. And I was filled with love for him. Then my love spread to other family members, and then to others not in my family, until, in ever-widening circles, it embraced the entire human race. Clearly, it was not so much *my* love as the expression of a vast and radiant Love at the heart of the universe. Bella was already *in* that Love—absorbed in that Love. She, and all of us, are that Love. It is the Source from which/whom we come and to which/whom we return. And, during our sojourn in this life, our task is to give expression to this Love.

As I emerged from this state, these words seemed clear to me: "We come from the One into the world of the Many, bearing love."

Last night I awakened from a dream pervaded by an unusual but powerful sense of *compassion*. The dream itself was quite bizarre, as dreams so often are. But on awakening, I was left with a profound sense of compassion for the characters in the dream. Since I was already awake, I went and sat in meditation, during which this pervasive sense of compassion grew deeper and stronger. It was another quite new experience among the many to which my grief has been opening me. Not so much a *feeling* of compassion as a compassionate *space* in which it was impossible to make any of my usual ego-driven judgments.

I felt hugely blessed to be in this space, but also sufficiently surprised to want to explore it. So I deliberately brought to mind those of whom I am usually very critical. Such as jihadists in the so-called Islamic State who decapitate their enemies without a hint of empathy. Or Donald Trump in his currently inflammatory bid to become the next President of the United States. And again to my surprise, I found it quite impossible to make any of my usual judgments. I was completely immersed in this compassionate space, from which I couldn't extricate myself even had I wanted to. Even this morning, its residue lingers. It remains to be seen how long it may continue.

Indeed, this space felt so unusual—in some sense so heavenly—that I wonder, somewhat anxiously, whether I am getting close to making my own exit from this life. There seems little doubt that some transformative process is

taking place in me—in its own time and not of my doing—
and that dying may be something like this.

Living as I do in a retirement village is attended by frequent
reminders of our mortality. Two nights ago, as I was arriving
home from an evening meeting, I was followed into the
village by a fire truck, which I then followed to see what was
happening. An ambulance was already at Carol and Neville's
townhouse, where Neville had just suffered a massive heart
attack. The paramedics succeeded in reviving his pulse, but
he had not regained consciousness when they lifted him
into the ambulance. Carol was distraught, and there was
nothing I could do but hold her.

The following morning, as I was making some online
travel arrangements, I felt prompted to phone Bella's
daughter, Shelley, at her vacation home in the Dominican
Republic. I rarely call Shelley, and never when she is on
vacation, but this seemed something I needed to do. When
she answered the phone, she was crying hysterically. Not
five minutes earlier, her father, who was visiting her, had
been accidentally struck by a car and instantly killed.

And then, that afternoon, while volunteering at the
hospice, I discovered that one of the patients—a relatively
young mother—was the daughter of a very dear friend and
someone I knew well. After a long struggle with cancer, she
was living her final days with enormous courage and grace.

There is so much sorrow and suffering in this world:
how can one not feel compassion? In my meditation last
night, recalling all that had happened, I thought of Shelley's
distress and easily came to tears. I imagined that Bella must
be feeling a hugely sorrowful love for Shelley, and seemed
to join with Bella in holding her in our love.

And then it dawned on me. Of course! We are all in
this together. In this often-painful, infinitely demanding,

one-semester course called "Learning to Love." And suffering is an integral part of the curriculum. In this school of hard knocks, life does not coddle us: it shatters us. It breaks us open, like a seed, in order that we may germinate and bear fruit. And because we are in this together, to have an open and compassionate heart means to *be* with one another—*No separation!*—in the midst of our suffering. This is what love is and what it does.

But it isn't just *my* love or *our* love. We are the more or less open, more or less constricted channels of a Love at the heart of the universe. Our compassion is but a faltering expression of the Big Love, the Great Heart, the Unnameable One that shares our pain and sorrow with infinite compassion. And holds us always in its embrace.

Perhaps the greatest change of all arises from knowing that none of these changes are a consequence of anything I have done. They are the accompaniments of an ongoing process beyond my control. Thankfully! Because I have no doubt that, if I tried to control the process or do it differently or shape it in any way, I would only mess it up. Though, upon reflection, I'm not sure it's possible to mess it up—at least not permanently. My life may be strewn with regrets. But even my screw-ups, born of self-willed efforts to make things happen the way I want them to, seem to get incorporated into this ongoing process. As if the process is self-correcting. A process that, despite myself, seems to carry me on its own trajectory, maybe over many lifetimes, on this often-painful journey that feels homeward bound.

In short, I am learning to *trust the process.*

The grief process itself has been so astonishing and unpredictable in the gifts it has delivered that I find myself surrendering more and more to its unfolding. Not trying to shape the process or determine its trajectory, but trusting it. And not the grief process only, but the entire process that is my life. Which in retrospect, as I reflect on its recurring themes, has bestowed more gifts than I could ever have imagined had I written the story myself.

Could I make this claim if, like so many, I had suffered the atrocities of war or the indignity of slavery or the horror of starvation? Or what so many, even in our privileged Western world, are required to endure? I have no answer for that. If my life story were written differently, who knows how its conclusion might read? But none of us escapes life's suffering. And what for me has, over these months since Bella died, made such a difference is discovering, at the intersection, when eternity invades the time-line of my story, that I am held in the embrace of a Presence. Borne up on an ocean of love. And that, even when the pain is greatest and my grief seems inconsolable, the process can be trusted. I can't justify that trust in any rational way. I can only testify to what I have known to be true.

But does *trusting* the process mean *surrendering* to it? My trust is usually conditional. I'm prepared to trust you, or the process, so long as my trust is justified. But if you let me down, or if the process gets too painful, then I'll intervene and, and in my own self-interest, take control again as best I can. Surrender, on the other hand, is unconditional. I relinquish all control. I let go. I surrender any attempt to shape the process or determine its outcome. Which is absurd. Who in their right mind would do that? Unless they were utterly defeated. I've always lived as if I am free to create my life and responsible for what I make of it. Congratulating myself when things go well, and always, with a kind of alertness bordering on anxiety, trying to ensure that everything works out the way I want it to. Wanting to extend my control, manage my world, reduce its uncertainties, and maximize my happiness.

But now I'm not so sure. I mean, I'm *really* not so sure. There seems to be a change occurring in me that has scarcely taken root. I only glimpse its possibility. The possibility of a whole new way of being in this world, based not on *control* but on *surrender*. A way of being that follows naturally from *living at the intersection*.

Certainly, whenever I have entered that blessed space, open to the Eternal, to the Wholly Present, to that inner realm where deep calls to deep, it is not because of anything that I have *done*. Always it feels like surrender. As if, despite myself, something in the region of my heart opens, and everything that feels like "me," with all its *doing* and trying to exercise some measure of control, dissolves into a vast inner spaciousness. Into an ocean of love that is itself unconditional.

Perhaps this is a key distinction between the vertical and horizontal planes, between the eternal and the space–time dimensions of my life. On the horizontal plane, in this world of "ten thousand things"° that seem so separate, everything is conditional. Everything is caused by something else. Here, in the realm of *It*, I too am a cause who must continually be *doing* something to make things happen as I wish. But on the vertical line, when in moments of connection I glimpse eternity, nothing is caused. How can anything be caused when there is no separation? Everything is unconditional. The love is unconditional. The trust is unconditional. And because there is nothing I need to make happen, the surrender too is unconditional.

How these two quite different ways of being come together at the intersection is something I can only glimpse. It cannot possibly mean that I no longer take action. The laundry must still be done, and dinner prepared, and the final chapter written. But the action need no longer be driven by any anxiety or any need to manage my world in an effort to ensure the future. Perhaps what is surrendered is just the perceived barrier of separation and the self-will required to maintain it. Is it possible simply to respond? To do only what love requires? To act without desire? Spontaneously and effortlessly in alignment with the natural flow of the universe? Perhaps that's what is meant by "going with the flow." Or what Lao Tzu meant when he wrote, enigmatically, "The Sage goes about doing nothing."° Or what Jesus was getting at when he repeatedly urged his followers not to be afraid: "Do not be anxious about your life. … Consider the lilies of the field."° Not that it was easy, even for him. Faced with imminent arrest and crucifixion, he sweated blood before he finally surrendered: "Not my will, but thine, be done."°

All this feels very new to me. I don't know where these inner changes will lead, but I am learning to trust the process. Please God, whatever life may yet deliver, may I always trust the process. With gratitude for those along the way who have encouraged me. Who, by finding words to share their own experience, have confirmed for me what I have glimpsed to be true. And who, often without their knowing it, have supported and encouraged me on my homeward journey.

One of these is Howard Thurman. He was the Dean of Marsh Chapel at Boston University when I was a graduate student there more than fifty years ago. I remember him as a big African-American whose size may have been less physical than an impression generated by his towering spiritual stature. In what little time I spent with him, I knew him to be a man of profound spiritual sensitivity who, from a place of deep inner calm, could take us in prayer and meditation to where I had never been before. Years later I came across a book titled *Deep Is the Hunger: Meditations by Howard Thurman*. It remains in my library as one of my best-loved volumes. Meditations by a man renowned as a social activist and civil rights leader who knew the meaning of surrender. The secret of what Taoists call *wu wei*, or "effortless action." Here is one of those meditations: I've turned to it so often that I've all but committed it to memory.

> My ego is like a fortress.
> I have built its walls stone by stone
> To hold out the invasion of the love of God.
> But I have stayed here long enough. There is light
> Over the barriers. O my God—
> The darkness of my house forgive
> And overtake my soul.
> I relax the barriers.
> I abandon all that I think I am,
> All that I hope to be,
> All that I believe I possess.
> I let go of the past,
> I withdraw my grasping hand from the future,
> And in the great silence of this moment,
> I alertly rest my soul.
> As the sea gull lays in the wind current,
> So I lay myself into the spirit of God.
> My dearest human relationships,
> My most precious dreams,
> I surrender to His care.
> All that I have called my own
> I give back. All my favorite things
> Which I would withhold in my storehouse

From His fearful tyranny,
I let go.
I give myself
Unto Thee, O my God.°

Amen! Thank you, Dr. Thurman. If what I am writing in this memoir touches anyone as I have been touched and blessed by what you and others have shared with me, I will be content.

~

I haven't seen my grandson Kai since we spent those few days together shortly after his birth. He's eighteen months old now, and I hope we'll have more time together soon. In the meantime, I'm enjoying the photos of him that his parents post on Facebook. In one, he's sitting in what looks like a highchair, a bottle clutched in his hands, his head tilted back, draining the last drops of whatever he's drinking. In his eyes I can see the first glimmers of independence. Just a hint of self-assertion that, over the next year, will blossom into his first full-throated "No!" His first outspoken objection to something he will not accept.

Although it typically heralds the onset of the "terrible twos," that first "No!" is an event to be celebrated. It marks the arrival of a separate individual, prepared to take a stand against what he or she finds undesirable. Which, in terms of healthy development, is exactly as it should be. Life requires that we erect a barrier of separation, expressed in this primeval "No," and so assert our individuality. Until, years later, we may reach a turning point. Prompted by our suffering, or infusions of grace, or just life's natural trajectory, we more and more risk saying "Yes!" Yes to the ongoing process. Yes to whatever life delivers. Yes to this "now" that can't be other than it is. Yes to the wonder and the mystery of it all.

We never spoke of it as such, but Bella learned this long before I did. Despite my years of meditation, I'm only a Johnny-come-lately. But Bella was a natural. Her whole life was "Yes!"

Will you marry me a second time? *Yes!*
Shall we make our home at Findhorn? *Yes!*
Will you be a vicar's wife in New Zealand? *Yes!*

Never a hint of objection. No anxiety. Without a moment's hesitation. No apparent need to push the world around. Had she found the secret of *wu wei*? Or was she, as she often said, when asked how she remained so calm in the midst of formidable catering events: "I'm like a duck. Calm on the surface. Paddling like hell underneath."

One of her favourite poems, from her dog-eared copy of Walt Whitman's *Leaves of Grass,* was "Song of the Open Road." And this final stanza in particular:

> Camerado, I give you my hand!
> I give you my love more precious than money,
> I give you myself before preaching or law;
> Will you give me yourself? will you come travel with me?
> Shall we stick by each other as long as we live?°

Yes! Yes! Yes! Thank you, my darling. Thank you so much for the unconditional "yes" that you said to me and to our life together. For trusting the process. Welcoming the changes. Allowing yourself to be carried on endless waves of transformation.

And the process continues. No beginning. No end. Born in eternity. Playing out in time. It doesn't matter what you call it. A *love story.* A *spiritual odyssey.* It's all the same. And we're all in it together. Devastated sometimes by the breaking of our hearts. Opening us to love. Calling us to surrender. To let go. Inviting us to live at the intersection. And bestowing on us gifts of grace we never thought possible.

If only I'd had the ears to hear, I swear I would have heard a resounding "Yes!" on the morning Bella died. When the cherry tree was in full bloom.

∾ EPILOGUE ∾

All that I have shared in this memoir is the truth and nothing but the truth. But it is not the whole truth. Not "warts and all," as Oliver Cromwell reportedly requested of his portrait painter.° My inner censor has wanted to ensure that no one's reputation is maligned and that Bella and I are presented in as favourable a light as possible.

That has not been difficult in my portrayal of Bella. Am I idolizing her? Perhaps. Though, in all honesty, there is nothing I can imagine saying about her that bears even a hint of criticism. Not so as regards myself. This memoir is a good deal less than "True Confessions." My foibles and my foolishness go far beyond anything that I have here reported. And that, it seems to me, is as it should be. Some things are better left unsaid.

My chief unease lies in sharing experiences that I know will be dismissed by some among my friends and family, and by many more among readers unknown to me, as nothing other than delusional—inventions of my grief-ravaged mind designed to deliver some small comfort. And they may be right. As noted in many of my journal entries, I am plagued by these same doubts myself. My sense of Bella's presence, the messages received as if from her in my practice of deep listening, those *moments of connection* when deep calls to deep and I find myself immersed in an ocean of love: all these immensely precious experiences feel so real and intuitively true that I am unable to simply dismiss them. Yet I know they cannot be supported by even a shred of empirical evidence—leaving me no option but to trust my experience as best I can, suffer my recurring doubts, and sometimes pray, "Lord, I believe. Help my unbelief."°

But I don't like being thought a fool. It may only be another of my ego-pretensions, but I've long thought of myself as intelligent, quite rational, and well educated. So to share experiences that many will doubtless regard as irrational if not delusional feels risky. Which brings me to the subject of this brief epilogue and to my hesitant decision now to relate one more experience that I have hitherto shared only with my closest friends.

It occurred on my 83rd birthday—just a month more than two years after Bella died. The retirement village in which I live marks residents' birthdays by treating them to a free Saturday-evening dinner. So, never one to turn down such an invitation, I was, at the appointed hour, duly seated in the beautiful dining room that stands at the centre of our village life.

As it turned out, I was the only person dining alone in a room buzzing with conversation and laughter from two large parties that were already under way. As many as sixteen people sat at one long refectory-style table, clearly enjoying whatever they were celebrating. Another party, some six or eight folk I didn't recognize, occupied a large round table. Unfortunately, both parties had arrived a few minutes before I had; thus, their orders had priority. I was told I could expect to wait up to half an hour before receiving my order. Which was fine by me. I wasn't going anywhere. So I ordered a rib-eye steak, medium-rare, and nursed a glass of Pinot Noir as I waited.

I could hear snippets of conversation from the two large dinner parties, but I wasn't paying attention. I was occupied with whatever musings come and go, of their own accord, when our minds are idling. I do remember, however, smiling to myself as I reflected on how unusual my situation was. I'm not accustomed to dining out alone, especially on my birthday. "So this is how it is," I thought. "Bella is gone. My family is scattered around the world. And here I am—alone." I wasn't feeling lonely. It just seemed humorously strange to find myself, on such an occasion, at this restaurant table by myself.

Close to thirty minutes must have passed in this state of reverie when, quite suddenly and to my utter astonishment, Bella was there. Straight ahead of me. Not more than six feet away. My own sweet darling. Of course I couldn't *see* her. But she was *there*. A distinct *presence*. I hadn't been aware of her presence for several months. I'd assumed she had "ascended." Or dissolved back into that ocean of love from which we have emerged. Perhaps nothing more now than a vestigial imprint on the fabric of eternity. Yet here she was. Unmistakably Bella. Not doing anything. Not saying anything.

Just *there*. Simply *present*. And she remained there, almost palpably present, for at least ten minutes. Even as Rocio, our dining-room hostess, served my dinner and I cut into a very tender rib-eye steak.

My own response was almost as surprising. No tears. Nothing I would identify as grief, or even the remnants of grief. Quite the contrary. I was smiling. Inwardly, almost casually, saying "Hi, love!" And thanking her for coming to be with me on my birthday. I was of course amazed by what was happening, but the whole experience had a certain "Of course!" feel to it. Of course, if anything of Bella remains in any sense *present*, where else would she want to be on my birthday? So "Thank you, love. Thank you for being here."

And so she remained. I would cut another piece of steak, and then look up, and she was still there. Until—and I remember this distinctly—she began to fade. And in just a few seconds she was gone. As if dissolving back into whatever that Reality is to which she now belongs.

What can I say? Still smiling, I felt immensely blessed. Immensely grateful.

And, of course, I am entirely capable of doubting the whole experience. Of dismissing it as wishful thinking. Of marvelling at what my mind is capable of concocting. I hasten to add this because I don't want anyone to think that I am easily deluded. Or, worse, perhaps a little crazy. I still want to be considered intelligent and rational. And with good reason, you might say, feeling hesitant to end this memoir by sharing this experience.

But my own reality is that, although I am quite unable to explain or make sense of this—and so many of the other experiences I have shared in this memoir—neither am I able to dismiss them. And if there's anything now that, in conclusion, I most want to share with you, dear reader, it's this: my unshakeable conviction, born of this most wondrous gift of a broken heart, that whoever you are, whatever your circumstances, and however painful your life may sometimes be, you are not alone. You are never alone. You are held, always and forever, in the intimate embrace of a love that will not let you go.

∼ NOTES ∼

FOREWORD

xvi **"The heart has its reasons":** Blaise Pascal, *Pascal's Pensées* (New York: E.P. Dutton, 1958), Section IV, "Of the Means of Belief," *Pensée number* 277.

xvi **"We know the truth":** Pascal, *Pensée number* 282.

INTRODUCTION: THEMES THAT SHAPE OUR STORY

1 **"One generation passes away, and another generation comes":** New King James Version of the Bible—Ecclesiastes 1:4,7.

2 **Nat King Cole's "Orange Colored Sky":** Written by Milton DeLugg and Willie Stein—Lyrics © AMY DEE MUSIC CORP. Nat King Cole's 1950 recording of the song is probably the best known.

2 **Perry Como's "Hot Diggity (Dog Ziggity Boom)":** Words written in 1956 by Al Hoffman and Dick Manning. Music written in 1883 by Emmanuel Chabrier. Recorded by Perry Como in 1956.

2 **"There is no soul":** Francis Crick (1916–2004) was a British molecular biologist and neuroscientist who codiscovered the structure of the DNA molecule in 1953 and subsequently, in 1962, was jointly awarded the Nobel Prize in Physiology or Medicine. The words attributed to him here are quoted by Antonio Damasio in "A Clear Consciousness," TIME Special Issue, Summer 1997/98, p. 74.

3 **"Ten thousand things":** Lao Tzu is the legendary founder of philosophical Taoism and the reputed author of the *Tao Te Ching*, usually dated to the 6th century BCE. His reference to the world of "ten thousand things" is from a translation of that work by Gia-Fu Feng and Jane English (New York: Vintage Books, 1972), Chapter 1, n.p.

3 **"A tale told by an idiot":** William Shakespeare, *Macbeth*, 5.5.26–28.

4 **Self-remembering:** A key concept in the spiritual psychology of G.I. Gurdjieff (1872–1949). Reference to it can be found in his *Views from the Real World: Early Talks of Gurdjieff* (New York: E.P. Dutton, 1973), pp. 79–80.

5 **"Blessed are those who mourn":** One of the Beatitudes attributed to Jesus, found in the Revised Standard Version of the Bible—Matthew 5:4.

5 **"I've been with many people":** Stephen Levine (1937–2016) was an American poet, author, and teacher of Theravada Buddhism who worked extensively with

the sick and dying. This quotation is from his book *Who Dies?: An Investigation of Conscious Living and Conscious Dying* (New York: Anchor Books, 1982), pp. 85–86.

6 **"There is a brokenness"**: An assistant to Elisabeth Kübler-Ross during the 1980s, Rashani Réa is a mother, a grief whisperer, a skilled carpenter and former potter, a passionate earth steward, and a prolific artist. After living in Europe for twenty-two years, she was called to the Big Island of Hawai'i, where she has spent the past twenty-six years co-creating two eco-sanctuaries in the remote district of Ka'u. She offers concerts, councils, kirtans, and retreats throughout the world and at her home, Kipukamaluhia Sanctuary. A strong and gentle eco-feminist voice in the interspiritual movement since 1986, Réa has recorded fifteen albums of "Soetry" (songs and poetry), published twenty-six books, and created an extensive collection of Dharma-Gaia greeting cards, incorporating words from contemporary and ancient mystics, mentors, poets, visionary pioneers, holy rebels, sages and teachers, woman-identified women, and singer/songwriters, from many different wisdom traditions. Her poem "The Unbroken" can be found on p. 171 of her book *Beyond Brokenness* (Bloomington, IN: Xlibris, 2009).

CHAPTER ONE: DAYS THAT CHANGE OUR LIFE

8 **I learned, for instance:** Bella's copy of Walt Whitman's *Leaves of Grass* is a Signet Classic edition (Toronto: New American Library, 1955).

8–9 **At the top of the first page:** What Bella inscribed in her copy of *Leaves of Grass* is her own variant of words from the King James Version of the Bible—Song of Solomon 2:8–12.

10 **A year earlier, Bella had come across:** Paul Hawken, *The Magic of Findhorn* (London: HarperCollins, 1975).

12 **"Life changes in the instant"**: Joan Didion (born 1934) is an acclaimed and extensively published American author and journalist. This quotation is from her book *The Year of Magical Thinking* (London: HarperCollins, 2005), p. 3.

12 **"Grief turns out to be a place"**: Didion, p. 188.

13 **"Be careful"**: Master Zhuang is traditionally considered to be the author of the *Chuang Tzu*—a work from China in the late 3rd century BCE. It and the *Tao Te Ching* are the two foundational texts of Taoism. This quotation is from Chapter 11, "On Letting Alone," in the translation by Herbert A. Giles (London: Bernard Quaritch, 1889).

13 **"The mind creates the abyss"**: Nisargadatta Maharaj, a 20th-century Indian guru, gained worldwide recognition when his talks were compiled and translated into English in a book titled *I Am That* (Mumbai: Chetana Publications, 1973). This quotation is from Jack Kornfield's book *A Path with Heart: A Guide Through the Perils and Promises of Spiritual Life* (New York: Bantam Books, 1993), p. 50.

13 **"Their hearts were torn open"**: Stephen Levine, *Who Dies?: An Investigation of Conscious Living and Conscious Dying* (New York: Anchor Books, 1982), p. 88.

13 **"The tearing open of the heart"**: Levine, p. 90.

13 **"It is in the tearing open of the heart"**: Levine, pp. 96–97.

CHAPTER TWO: THE MORNING BELLA DIED

18 *The Tibetan Book of the Dead:* An English translation of the Tibetan *Bardo Thodol,* by Walter Evans-Wentz (Oxford: Oxford University Press, 1927).

18 **Confirmed by those who've had a near-death experience:** For detailed descriptions of such experiences, see, for example, Kenneth Ring's *Lessons from the Light: What We Can Learn from the Near-Death Experience* (Needham, MA: Moment Point Press, 1998).

19 **"Cross over now, beloved one":** Rashani Réa, *Beyond Brokenness* (Bloomington, IN: Xlibris, 2009), p. 159. See Notes to Introduction for biographical details.

20 **"These eyes are not you":** Réa, pp. 203–204.

23 **"To never have been born":** From Antigone, a play written in 441 BCE by Greek tragedian Sophocles (496–406 BCE).

24 **"To love ... is to be vulnerable":** British novelist and academic C.S. Lewis (1898–1963) married Joy Davidman Gresham in 1956; shortly afterward, she was diagnosed with terminal bone cancer. Following her death in 1960, he wrote an intensely personal account of his bereavement (under the pseudonym N.W. Clerk): *A Grief Observed* (London: Faber & Faber, 1961). In the same year as her death, he published *The Four Loves* (London: Geoffrey Bles, 1960), in which this quotation appears on p. 121.

24 **"My heart has become an ocean":** British-born Pir Vilayat Inayat Khan (1916–2004) succeeded his father, Hazrat Inayat Khan, as spiritual leader of the Sufi Order in the West. This quotation is from "Sayings of Pir-o-Murshid Inayat Khan," found online at https://wahiduddin.net/mv2/say/vadan_alankaras.htm.

CHAPTER THREE: "IN THE MIDST OF LIFE WE ARE IN DEATH"

27 **According to the *Warren Commission Report*:** Precisely when President John F. Kennedy was pronounced dead is recorded in *The Warren Commission Report,* Chapter 1: Summary and Conclusions, p. 4, found online at https://www.archives.gov/research/jfk/warren-commission-report/chapter-1.html.

29 **"Death is sitting next to you":** Carlos Castaneda, *The Teachings of Don Juan: A Yaqui Way of Knowledge* (Oakland, CA: University of California Press, 1968).

29 **"In the midst of life we are in death":** From "The Order for the Burial of the Dead" in *The Book of Common Prayer,* originally published in 1549. Currently translated into more than 150 languages, it is used by churches around the world, both within and without the Anglican Communion.

34 **"We'll Meet Again":** A 1939 song made famous by Vera Lynn, with music and lyrics composed and written by Ross Parker and Hughie Charles.

34–35 **"For everything there is a season":** Revised Standard Version of the Bible—Ecclesiastes 3:1–2.

35 **"All the world's a stage":** William Shakespeare, *As You Like It,* 2.7.138–140.

36 **"Today is a good day to die":** An account of this statement's origins is given by Takatoka in a Manataka American Indian Council publication, found online at http://manataka.org/page1909.html.

CHAPTER FOUR: "IS THAT YOU, DARLING?"

38 **Fifty years ago:** Elisabeth Kübler-Ross (1926–2004) was a Swiss-born American psychiatrist who pioneered near-death studies. She introduced her now-famous theory of the five stages of grief in her book *On Death and Dying: What the Dying Have to Teach Doctors, Nurses, Clergy and Their Own Families* (New York: Simon and Schuster, 1969).

41 **I kept all these things and pondered them in my heart:** Paraphrased from the King James Version of the Bible—Luke 2:19.

42 **"The Lord bless you and keep you":** Revised Standard Version of the Bible— Numbers 6:24–26.

43 **O Lord, support us all the day long of this troublous life:** My own variant of a prayer ascribed to John Henry Newman (1801–1890), an Anglican priest who later became a Roman Catholic Cardinal.

43 **"Earth to earth, ashes to ashes":** From a revised edition of "The Order for the Burial of the Dead" in the *Book of Common Prayer* (Oxford: Oxford University Press, 1928).

44 **"Why do you seek the living among the dead?":** New King James Version of the Bible—Luke 24:5.

CHAPTER FIVE: NO SEPARATION

51 **"I do my thing, and you do your thing":** Frederick S. ("Fritz") Perls, *Gestalt Therapy Verbatim* (Gouldsboro, ME: Gestalt Journal Press, 1992), p. 24. Originally published in 1969.

53 **It's *like* a grain of mustard seed:** Jesus' parables of the mustard seed and of the leaven are found in all versions of the Bible—Matthew 13:31–33.

54 **Or, in the language of Martin Buber:** Buber describes his distinction between *I–It* and *I–Thou* throughout his book *I and Thou*, 2nd edition, translated by Ronald Gregor Smith (New York: Charles Scribner's Sons, 1958). Originally published in German as *Ich und Du* in 1923.

56 **"Ten thousand things":** Lao Tzu, *Tao Te Ching*, translated by Gia-Fu Feng and Jane English (New York: Vintage Books, 1972), Chapter 1, n.p. See also the reference to Lao Tzu in the Notes for the Introduction.

CHAPTER SIX: SHADES OF GREY

57 **Like Archimedes:** Archimedes (287–212 BCE) was a Greek mathematician and physicist. His "eureka moment" reportedly occurred while he was bathing. What became known as Archimedes' Principle is defined by the *Encyclopedia Britannica* in this way: "Any body completely or partially submerged in a fluid (gas or liquid) at rest is acted upon by an upward, or buoyant, force the magnitude of which is equal to the weight of the fluid displaced by the body." Found online at https://www.britannica.com/science/Archimedes-principle.

58 **Most recently, immersed in the thinking of theoretical physicists:** Theoretical

physicists espousing the idea that consciousness may be a fundamental feature of reality include David Bohm (1917–1992), Bernard d'Espagnat (1921–2015), Sir Roger Penrose (born 1931), Amit Goswami (born 1936), and Nick Herbert (born 1936).

60 **"Most fortunate of all are those who are not yet born":** New Living Translation of the Bible—Ecclesiastes 4:3.

61 *Information* **belongs to the essential nature of reality:** Among scientists currently arguing this, one is physicist Craig Hogan, Director of the Fermilab Center for Particle Astrophysics near Chicago, Illinois. Reporting on Hogan's thinking, in an article titled "Is Space Digital?" (*Scientific American*, February 2012, Vol. 306, No. 2, pp. 30–36), Michael Moyer wrote: "Physicists have, over the past couple of decades, uncovered profound insights into how the universe stores information— even going so far as to suggest that information, not matter and energy, constitutes the most basic unit of existence."

62 **One is Robert Lanza:** Robert Lanza (born 1956) is an American biologist and pioneer in stem cell research, serving as Chief Scientific Officer of the Astellas Institute for Regenerative Medicine in Marlborough, Massachusetts. His claim that consciousness exists outside the constraints of space and time is set out in "A New Theory of the Universe," *The American Scholar* (01 March 2007), found online at https://theamericanscholar.org/a-new-theory-of-the-universe/#; *Biocentrism: How Life and Consciousness Are the Keys to Understanding the True Nature of the Universe* (Dallas, TX: BenBella Books, 2009); and most recently in *Beyond Biocentrism: Rethinking Time, Space, Consciousness, and the Illusion of Death* (Dallas, TX: BenBella Books, 2016).

62–63 **Another was German physicist Hans-Peter Dürr:** Quoted in Janey Tracey, "Physicists Claim That Consciousness Lives in Quantum State After Death," *Outer Places*, 17 June 2014. Found online at http://www.outerplaces.com/science/item/4518-physicists-claim-that-consciousness-lives-in-quantum-state-after-death.

66 **To prepare for our Sunday Gathering:** The Sunday Gathering is a group of assorted humanists, agnostics, sometime-Buddhists, and renegades from institutional religion who have been meeting once a month in Christchurch, New Zealand, for more than twenty years to share and support one another in their spiritual journey.

67 **Albert Camus' sense of "the Absurd":** French philosopher Albert Camus (1913–1960) introduced his concept of "the Absurd" in his philosophical essay *Le Mythe de Sisyphe* (Paris: Éditions Gallimard, 1942). The English translation by Justin O'Brien, *The Myth of Sisyphus*, was first published in 1955 (London: Hamish Hamilton).

67 **Jean-Paul Sartre's "nausea":** Sartre (1905–1980) was a French existentialist philosopher, playwright, and novelist. His philosophical novel *Nausea* (or *La Nausée*), first published in 1938, fleshes out one of his core ideas—that "life begins on the other side of despair." (See the analysis of *Nausea* titled "Depression and Expression: Life Begins on the Other Side of Despair," by Ann McCulloch with Aliki Pavlou, found online at http://www.doubledialogues.com/article/depression-and-expression-life-begins-on-the-other-side-of-despair/.)

67 **"The raft to be abandoned upon reaching the other shore":** A traditional Buddhist saying, quoted in Jennifer Sumison, *An Exploration of Eastern Philosophy: Enhancing Understanding of Reflection*. Paper presented at the Annual Conference of the Australian Association for Research in Education, Newcastle, November 1994. Found online at https://www.aare.edu.au/data/publications/1994/sumsj94204.pdf.

68 **What Martin Buber called "the inexpressible confirmation of meaning'":** Expanding on what he calls "the inexpressible confirmation of meaning" that accompanies the I–Thou relation, Buber wrote: "Meaning is assured. Nothing can ever longer be meaningless. The question about the meaning of life is no longer there. … You do not know how to exhibit and define the meaning of life, you have no formula or picture for it, yet it has more certitude for you than the perceptions of your senses." *I and Thou*, 2nd edition, translated by Ronald Gregor Smith (New York: Charles Scribner's Sons, 1958), p. 110.

68–69 **And then, in December 1273:** St. Thomas Aquinas' mystical experience in the Chapel of St. Nicholas is described by Brian Davies in *The Thought of Thomas Aquinas* (Oxford: Oxford University Press, 1993), p. 9.

CHAPTER SEVEN: "WHAT IS THIS THING CALLED LOVE?"

71 **"What Is This Thing Called Love?":** Written in 1929 by American composer and songwriter Cole Porter (1891–1964) for the musical *Wake Up and Dream*.

73 **"Our normal waking consciousness":** William James, *The Varieties of Religious Experience: A Study in Human Nature* (New York: Penguin Classics, 1985), p. 388. Originally published in 1902.

74 **"God is love":** Found in all versions of the Bible—1 John 4:8.

75–76 **There is a book of poetry, still in my library:** American anthropologist Edmund Carpenter (1922–2011) translated "Great sea sends me drifting" and other Inuit poems in *Anerca* (Toronto: J.M. Dent & Sons, 1972). Originally published in 1959.

79 **Jenny Wade … has studied this phenomenon:** Jenny Wade, *Transcendent Sex: When Lovemaking Opens the Veil* (New York: Paraview Books, 2004).

79 **"When we make love, it's like I disappear":** Quoted in Harry Maurer, *Sex: An Oral History* (Hawthorn, Australia: Penguin Books Australia, 1994), p. 456.

79 **"There is a unitive energy":** Quoted in Jalaja Bonheim, *Aphrodite's Daughters: Women's Sexual Stories and the Journey of the Soul* (New York: Simon & Schuster, 1997), pp. 40–41.

CHAPTER EIGHT: "ON THAT BUMPY ROAD TO LOVE"

83 **"We may never, never meet again":** From "They Can't Take That Away from Me," written by Ira Gershwin (lyrics) and George Gershwin (music) for the 1937 film *Shall We Dance*. Reprinted with permission: see copyright page (p. iv) for details.

84 **Claudio Naranjo:** A Chilean-born American psychiatrist (born 1932) who is considered a pioneer in integrating psychotherapy and the spiritual traditions.

85 **Maharishi Mahesh Yogi:** An Indian spiritual teacher (1918–2008) who developed and taught the practice known as Transcendental Meditation.

86 **"The two shall become one":** Revised Standard Version of the Bible—Matthew 19:5.

89, 90 **"The Way We Were":** Written by Alan Bergman, Marilyn Bergman, and Marvin Hamlisch for the 1973 film of the same title. The song was first recorded by the movie's star, Barbra Streisand.

90 **"What therefore God has joined together, let no man put asunder":** Revised Standard Version of the Bible—Matthew 19:6.

93 **"He learned ... through what he suffered":** Revised Standard Version of the Bible—Hebrews 5:8.

CHAPTER NINE: HOMEWARD BOUND

95 *Journey of Awakening:* Subtitled *A Meditator's Guide Book*, written by Ram Dass (born 1931). Revised edition (New York: Bantam, 1990). Originally published in 1978.

95 *Self-remembering:* G.I. Gurdjieff, *Views from the Real World: Early Talks of Gurdjieff* (New York: E.P. Dutton, 1973), pp. 79–80.

95 *Toward the One:* Written by Sufi spiritual teacher Vilayat Inanyat Khan (1916–2004). (New York: Harper & Row, 1974).

95 **"Every animal ... needs to set its body apart":** Frans de Waal, *Are We Smart Enough to Know How Smart Animals Are?* (New York: W.W. Norton, 2016), p. 240. de Waal (born 1948) is a Dutch-born American primatologist who has written several books about primate social behaviour.

96 **"Ten thousand things":** Lao Tzu, *Tao Te Ching*, translated by Gia-Fu Feng and Jane English (New York: Vintage Books, 1972), Chapter 1, n.p. See also the reference to Lao Tzu in the Notes for the Introduction.

96 **When, in Martin Buber's terms:** Buber describes his distinction between *I–It* and *I–Thou* throughout his book *I and Thou*, 2nd edition, translated by Ronald Gregor Smith (New York: Charles Scribner's Sons, 1958). Originally published in German as *Ich und Du* in 1923.

96 **"He who is to be made to dwindle":** Lao Tzu, Chapter 36, "The Rhythm of Life," *The Wisdom of Laotse*, translated by Lin Yutang (New York: Modern Library, 1948), p. 191. See also the reference to Lao Tzu in the Notes for the Introduction.

96 **"A human being is part of the whole":** Attributed to physicist Albert Einstein (1879–1955); quoted in Ken Wilber, *Up from Eden: A Transpersonal View of Human Evolution* (Boulder, CO: Shambala, 1983), p. 6.

97 **"Beloved, let us love one another":** Revised Standard Version of the Bible—1 John 4:7.

98 **"Jesus' Parable of the Prodigal Son":** Revised Standard Version of the Bible—Luke 15:11–24.

99   *The Practice of the Presence of God:* Collected teachings of Brother Lawrence (1605–1691), a 17th-century Carmelite monk (Peabody, MA: Hendrickson, 2011).

99   **Nikolai Berdyaev:** Russian existentialist philosopher (1874–1948). For a representative text, see his *Spirit and Reality* (London: Geoffrey Bles, 1939).

100   **"To see a World in a Grain of Sand":** From the poem "Auguries of Innocence," by William Blake (1757–1827).

100   **"And I have felt / a presence":** From the poem "Lines Written a Few Miles Above Tintern Abbey," by William Wordsworth (1770–1850).

102   **"Sweat broke out on my forehead":** Ram Dass, "Chapter 1: Journey," *Be Here Now* (San Cristobal, NM: Lama Foundation, 1971).

CHAPTER TEN: INNER CONNECTIONS

106   **Then one day, in a Greensboro bookshop:** The first book Bella picked up was Barbara Friedlander's *The Findhorn Cookbook: An Approach to Cooking with Consciousness* (New York: Penguin, 1976).

106   **But, as she returned it to the shelf:** The book that accidentally fell at Bella's feet was Paul Hawken's *The Magic of Findhorn* (New York: HarperCollins, 1975).

111   **"This is the judgment, that the light has come":** Revised Standard Version of the Bible—John 3:19.

113   **"Let Hertz put you in the driver's seat":** For a 1964 version of this TV ad, see https://www.youtube.com/watch?v=GLpNmuPQE94.

113   **I remember thinking at the time:** *Animal Farm* is an allegorical novella satirizing the Soviet Union's Stalinist era. Written by George Orwell (1903–1950), it was first published in London, by Secker and Warburg, in 1945.

CHAPTER ELEVEN: SECOND DEATH

117   **"Everything flows":** A quotation famously attributed to Heraclitus by Plato in Section 402a of his dialogue *Cratylus*. Heraclitus (535–475 BCE) was a pre-Socratic philosopher from the city of Ephesus, then part of the Persian Empire and now in Turkey.

118   **"I don't believe in an afterlife":** K. Mitch Hodge, Paulo Sousa, and Claire White, "Proposed Cognitive Mechanisms and Representational Structures of Afterlife Beliefs: A Review" (2015), found online at http://www.academia.edu/335041/Cognitive_Foundations_of_Afterlife_Beliefs.

119   **Exploring more of what Mitch ... had written:** K. Mitch Hodge, "The Death We Fear Is Not Our Own: Revisiting and Reframing the Folk Psychology of Souls" (2016), found online at http://www.academia.edu/11755027/The_Death_We_Fear_is_Not_Our_Own_Revisiting_and_Reframing_the_Folk_Psychology_of_Souls.

124–125 **The strange New Testament reports of Jesus' resurrection and ascension:** Revised Standard Version of the Bible—Acts 1:3, Luke 24:51, and Acts 1:9. Biblical references to the number forty are not to be taken literally. They indicate an indefinite or uncertain period of time—as in the forty days Noah spent riding out the flood, the forty years during which the Israelites wandered in the desert before reaching the Promised Land, the forty days that Jesus spent in the wilderness facing his temptations, and the forty days during which he appeared to his disciples after his death and before he was parted from them.

126 *The Portrait of a Lady:* A 1996 film adaptation of Henry James's novel of the same name. The movie was directed by New Zealand filmmaker Dame Jane Campion.

128 **In the Bible, it is epitomized by Abraham:** The Biblical patriarch Abraham is identified as an exemplar of faith by St. Paul in his letter to the Hebrews 11:8. The quotation here is from the Revised Standard Version of the Bible.

CHAPTER TWELVE: WHEN "DEEP CALLS TO DEEP"

129 **"Onward, Christian Soldiers":** A 19th-century English hymn. Sabine Baring-Gould wrote the lyrics in 1865, and Arthur Seymour Sullivan composed the music in 1872.

129 **"Courage, Brother, Do Not Stumble":** A 19th-century English hymn. Its lyrics were written by Norman MacLeod in 1857, and its music was composed by Arthur Seymour Sullivan in 1871.

131 **"Deep calls to deep at the thunder of thy cataracts":** Revised Standard Version of the Bible—Psalms 42:7.

133 **"The dynamic Spiritual Heart"** and **"you can learn to find the Self":** Quotations attributed to the Indian Hindu sage Bhagavan Sri Ramana Maharshi (1879–1950). Found online at https://hridaya-yoga.com/hridaya-yoga-articles/what-is-hridaya-the-spiritual-heart/.

135 **"Ten thousand things":** Lao Tzu, *Tao Te Ching*, translated by Gia-Fu Feng and Jane Jane English (New York: Vintage Books, 1972), Chapter 1, n.p. See also the reference to Lao Tzu in the Notes for the Introduction.

137 **"Cease from practice based on intellectual understanding":** Response by 13th-century Japanese Buddhist poet Dōgen Zenji (1200–1253), to the Zen koan "What is your original face before your parents were born?" Found online at https://www.dailyzen.com/quotes/cease-practice.

139 **I recently shared some of these experiences:** Kenneth Ring (born 1936) is Professor Emeritus of Psychology at the University of Connecticut, cofounder and past president of the International Association for Near-Death Studies, and founding editor of its quarterly publication, the *Journal of Near-Death Studies*. He wrote the foreword for this book: further biographical information can be found there (on p. xiii).

139–140 **"There are moments of silent depth":** Martin Buber, *I and Thou*, 2nd edition, translated by Ronald Gregor Smith (New York: Charles Scribner's Sons, 1958), pp. 31–33.

CHAPTER THIRTEEN: LIVING AT THE INTERSECTION

142 **"Ten thousand things"**: Lao Tzu, *Tao Te Ching*, translated by Gia-Fu Feng and Jane Jane English (New York: Vintage Books, 1972), Chapter 1, n.p. See also the reference to Lao Tzu in the Notes for the Introduction.

144 **"Two poles of humanity"**: Martin Buber, *I and Thou*, translated by Ronald Gregor Smith (New York: Charles Scribner's Sons, 1958), p. 65.

144 **"The world of It"**: Buber, p. 100.

144 **"It is not possible to live in the bare present"**: Buber, p. 34.

144 **Self-remembering:** G.I. Gurdjieff, *Views from the Real World: Early Talks of Gurdjieff* (New York: E.P. Dutton, 1973), pp. 79–80.

145 **"After enlightenment, the laundry"**: A Zen proverb found online at http://think exist.com/quotation/after_enlightenment-the_laundry/253201.html.

145 **"Ten thousand things"**: Lao Tzu, Chapter 1, n.p.

145 **"Loved ... and lost awhile"**: From the hymn "Lead, Kindly Light. Words written in 1883 by John Henry Newman. Music written in 1865 by John Bacchus Dykes.

146 **"We're born alone, we live alone, we die alone"**: Attributed to American actor and writer Orson Welles (1915–1985). Found online at www.bornalone.org.

146 **"The Tao that can be named is not the eternal Tao"**: Lao Tzu, Chapter 1, n.p.

146–147 **"Don't try to name it"**: Stephen Levine, *A Year to Live: How to Live This Year As If It Were Your Last* (New York: Three Rivers Press, 1997), p. 116.

147 **"The inexpressible confirmation of meaning"**: Buber, p. 110.

147 **"Nothing can any longer be meaningless"**: Buber, p. 110.

148 **Kierkegaard's "despair"**: Danish existentialist philosopher Søren Kierkegaard (1813–1855) presented his concept of existential despair in *The Sickness unto Death* (Belmont, NC: Wiseblood Classics, 2013); originally published in 1849.

148 **Camus' sense of "the Absurd"**: French philosopher Albert Camus (1913–1960) introduced his concept of "the Absurd" in his philosophical essay *Le Mythe de Sisyphe* (Paris: Éditions Gallimard, 1942). The English translation by Justin O'Brien, *The Myth of Sisyphus*, was first published in 1955 (London: Hamish Hamilton).

148 **"Man's search for meaning"**: Austrian psychiatrist and Holocaust survivor Viktor Frankl (1905-1997) wrote *Man's Search for Meaning: An Introduction to Logotherapy* (Boston: Beacon, 2006); originally published in German in 1946 (under a title that translates as "To Nevertheless Say 'Yes' to Life: A Psychologist Experiences the Concentration Camps"), and in English in 1959.

149 *Brooklyn*: A 2015 British–Canadian–Irish film directed by John Crowley (20th Century Fox/Fox Searchlight). Available on DVD.

154 **"Ten thousand things"**: Lao Tzu, Chapter 1, n.p.

154 **"The Sage goes about doing nothing"**: Lao Tzu, Chapter 2, n.p.

154 **"Do not be anxious about your life"**: Revised Standard Version of the Bible— Matthew 6:25, 28.

154 **"Not my will, but thine, be done"**: Revised Standard Version of the Bible— Luke 22:42.

155–156 **"My ego is like a fortress":** Howard Thurman (1899–1981), *Deep Is the Hunger: Meditations by Howard Thurman* (New York: Harper, 1951), pp. 201–202.

157 **"Song of the Open Road":** Walt Whitman, *Leaves of Grass* (Toronto: New American Library, 1955), pp. 136–144.

EPILOGUE

159 **Not "warts and all":** For a discussion of the likelihood that Cromwell actually issued this instruction to his portraitist, Sir Peter Lely, see https://www.phrases .org.uk/meanings/warts-and-all.html.

159 **"Lord, I believe":** Modern English Version of the Bible—Mark 9:24.

Made in the USA
Middletown, DE
19 October 2018